Every Christian a Counselor

Dr. Nicolas Ellen

Every Christian a Counselor

Readers may order copies by visiting www.mycounselingcorner.com

Published and Printed By Expository Counseling Center
Houston, Texas

Unless otherwise noted, scripture references are taken from the New American Standard Bible. © The Lockman Foundation, 1960, 1962, 1963, 1968, 1971, 1972, 1973, 1975, 1977.

Publisher's Cataloging in Publication
Ellen, Nicolas*: Every Christian a Counselor*
1. Counseling 2. Psychology 3. Christianity 4. Discipleship

ISBN 978-0-9779693-5-7

TABLE OF CONTENTS

INTRODUCTION

Has the Church met its match? Does the Church lack the tools to handle the relational, social, and emotional issues of this present evil age? Are we really competent to counsel? It is not uncommon for people to reduce the church to a place of learning instead of place of transformation. But why? I believe it is because we are not organized and functioning as a God-empowered community that helps people live the truth. As a result, "the real problems" people encounter are deferred to the secular priest of our culture. The Church has been called and equipped to be a community where one learns the truth and is transformed by it. The Church has been called and equipped to counsel "the real problems" of this present evil age. Andrew Peters, a professor of pastoral counseling, made the point that we don't need "something more" we need "more of something." The point is we don't need something more than the Word of God to help deal with the issues of our day. We need more of the Word of God to deal with our issues of the day. We don't need something more than the church to handle the relational, social, or emotional ills of this present evil age. We need more of the church! We need the church to function as God intended so that He can work through it accordingly. This will result in a church honoring God through genuine evangelism and discipleship as we are called and equipped to do.

But what about counseling? Is the Church able to counsel these problems we so often see today? Is that the role of the Church? Shouldn't the church leave the work of counseling to the professionals of this world? True genuine counseling is the work of the Church. Counseling that transforms lives comes from a God-empowered community. Counseling that transforms lives comes through a Church that is organized and functioning as God intended.

A church that is God-honoring functions as an instrument of God. Counseling that is God-honoring functions as an instrument of the church. The role of counseling is directly related to the work of the church just as the work of the church is directly related to the work of God. In order for a church to function as an instrument of God and counseling to function as instrument of the church, the church must operate in correspondence to the work of God in the world. Therefore, we must learn the work of God in the world in order to understand how the church and counseling should functions as instruments of God in that work. The key point to consider is that God is saving souls from the penalty, the power, the presence of sin and maturing saints into the image of Jesus Christ.

Since God is saving souls from the consequences of sin and sanctifying saints into the likeness of Jesus Christ, everything the church does must correspond to this work of God. God's solution to man's problems is summed up in salvation and sanctification. Man cannot live as God designed without being delivered from sin and being sanctified in Jesus Christ. Every problem of man can be traced back to sin. Therefore, a life lived apart from God is a life that is lived in futility and destined for destruction. As God saves souls from the consequences of sin and sanctifies man into the likeness of Jesus Christ, He uses the church through the work of evangelism and discipleship to accomplish His work of salvation and sanctification.

Therefore, the local church must structure itself in such a manner that she can facilitate the work of evangelism and discipleship in a effective, efficient and orderly manner. In the book of Acts we find that the Church functioned in a manner that seemed to be effective, efficient, and orderly in relation to the work of evangelism and discipleship. As we evaluate some of the activities of first church in the Book of Acts, we will identify some key principles to consider for organizing and structuring the church for the work of evangelism and discipleship.

Steve Viars says "You can't have an effective counseling ministry until you have a ministry that counsels." In other words, a church that is not functioning effectively, efficiently, and orderly in the work of evangelism and discipleship cannot have a counseling ministry that functions as God intended. Therefore, we must understand and develop a church that counsels via evangelism and discipleship before we can have an effective counseling ministry.

As God is saving souls and maturing saints into the image of Jesus Christ through the work of evangelism and discipleship, we must understand the phases of change, the stages of spiritual growth, areas where change is to take place and how the Word of God is used in connection with this insight in the work of evangelism and discipleship.

As we develop a church that is committed, organized, and structured around evangelism and discipleship, we can have an effective counseling ministry. Since the work of evangelism and discipleship is done effectively and efficiently through interpersonal relationships, we must build our relationships with that in mind. As we develop interpersonal relationships, we must consider that we are ambassadors to unbelievers with the primary objective of presenting the gospel to unbelievers. We must also consider that we are builders of believers with the primary objective of helping believers become like Christ in all aspects to spiritual maturity.

If sin is not man's problem then the person and work of Jesus of Christ is not the solution. We know from Scripture that sin is man's essential problem of life. God's solution to man's essential problem of sin is summed up in the work of salvation and sanctification. Biblical counseling is the work of evangelism and discipleship on a one on one basis starting with identifying the problem and using the Word of God to work through the solution of salvation or sanctification according to the need of the moment as God wills. Therefore, genuine biblical counseling is an avenue whereby evangelism and discipleship takes place on an interpersonal level as the Word of God is used within the context it was written to address the problems and concerns of individuals anticipating the salvation of sinners and the sanctification of Saints, as God wills. Every Christian is called to the work of evangelism and discipleship, which means every Christian is a counselor!

EVERY CHRISTIAN A COUNSELOR
A FIRM FOUNDATION (PART 1)
CHAPTER 1

A church that is God-honoring functions as an instrument of God. Counseling that is God-honoring functions as an instrument of the church. The relationship between counseling and the church is inseparable. The role of counseling is directly related to the work of the church just as the work of the church is directly related to the work of God. In order for a church to function as an instrument of God and counseling to function as instrument of the church, the church must operate in correspondence to the work of God in the world. Therefore, we must learn the work of God in the world in order to understand how the church and counseling should functions as instruments of God in that work. The key point to consider is that God is saving souls from the penalty, the power, and the presence of sin and maturing saints into the image of Jesus Christ.

The Definition and Consequences of Sin

The problem in this world is sin. Sin can be defined as doing what God has commanded us not to do. Do you remember the rhyme "Mary, Mary quite contrary"? All of us are like Mary; we tend to do the opposite of what God commands us to do. Sin is also not doing what God has command us to do. Think of the Ten Commandments. All of us have broken the Ten Commandments in one way or another in thoughts, words, or actions. In essence, sin is missing the mark as well transgressing the standards set by God. We have not become or done what God has commanded. We have chosen to become and do what God has forbidden. Consequently, we have negative results in our lives.

Sin has lead to severe consequences for mankind. For instance, sin has separated and alienated mankind from God (Ephesians 2:11-12). It put a dividing line between us and God. Man no longer seeks after God as he did in the garden. Sin also has led to mankind worshipping self above God (Romans 1:18-32, 2 Timothy 3:1-5, Luke 12:13-21). The most important person to man is himself as a result of sin. Man believes life revolves around himself instead of God. What's even worse is that sin has led mankind to worship the creation above God. Man no longer seeks to manage creation for the glory

9

of God. Man now seeks to own creation for the glory of self. Overall, we see the terrible reality that sin has corrupted one's thinking about himself and the use of the world. All are guilty of sin indirectly and directly as a result of the sin of Adam. Indirectly, mankind was imputed with sin (Romans 5:12-21, 3:10). This means that mankind is placed in the position of sinner before God. He is identified with Adam as a sinner. In addition, mankind is born with inherited sin indirectly because of the sin of Adam (Psalm 51:5, Jeremiah 17:9, Genesis 6:5, Matthew 15:15-20, Romans 8:7, Romans 7:7-24). The sin seed of Adam is now the heart condition of all mankind born after him. In other words, all are born with a evil nature because Adam's sin brought corruptness to all born after him. Moreover, as a result of imputed and inherited sin, man directly walks in individual sin before God and with others (Romans 3:10-18, 23, Ecclesiastes 7:20, Romans 8:5-8). His position and condition of sin leads to a life of sin. His life is committed to self. In summary, man is born with sin and lives in sin because of the sin of Adam.

Mankind now experiences death on three levels as result of Adam's sin in the garden. First, mankind experiences spiritual death (Ephesians 2:1-5). This is a separation from the influence of God's power, presence, and promises. It is a separation from the fellowship and communion with God. Second, mankind experiences physical death (James 2:26). This is when the spirit of man is separated from the physical body. This separation happens when physical life ceases. Third, mankind experiences eternal death (Revelation 20:4-15, John 3:16-18). At this point man is separated from God forever after physical death. The separation from God is unto eternal punishment in the lake of fire for ever. Adam's disconnect from God became mankind's separation from God.

The Gospel and the Benefits to Mankind

God the Father made provision for the sins of mankind through the finished work of Jesus Christ (Ephesians 2:1-10). Jesus Christ who is God and the Son of God took on the form of man (John 1:14-18). Imagine this reality. God allowed Himself to take on the form of man!

Jesus Christ took on the form of man so that He may pay the penalty for sins of the human race (Hebrews 10:1-18). Nothing other than God Himself could pay the debt. It took the Eternal God to pay for the Eternal wage that sin brings. Through Christ's physical death on the Cross, literal burial and resurrection from physical death, Jesus paid the penalty for all sins committed by mankind (Acts 2:22-36). Past, present, and future sins have been paid for. God the Father poured His wrath on God the Son to pay for our sin debt. There is no greater love than this!

Through the finished work of Jesus Christ mankind can be saved from the consequences of sin. First, through Christ's physical death on the Cross, literal burial, and resurrection from physical death, man can be delivered from the penalty of sin (Romans 6:1-15). He can be set free from paying the debt owed from sin. Man can literally be debt free as it relates to sin. Second, through Christ's physical death on the Cross, literal burial and resurrection from physical death, man can be delivered from the power of sin (Revelation 21:1-27). He can have the ability to overcome sin. Man can have the ability to resist the evil from within and without. Third, through Christ's physical death on the Cross, literal burial and resurrection from physical death, man can be delivered from the presence of sin in the future to come. Mankind can one day walk in the presence of God without sin being presence. He can be freed from the very presence of sin because of the work Jesus Christ. All of this is possible as a result of the Person and work of Jesus Christ.

The Right Response to the Gospel and the Result of that Response

A right response to the finished work of Jesus Christ will result in salvation from the penalty, power, and one day presence of sin unto a new and right relationship God. The first step towards deliverance from the consequences of your sin is to acknowledge to God that you recognize that you are a sinner that deserves punishment for your sin, and that you realize you need to be forgiven of your sin. One cannot be delivered if he does not recognize the need. Once you come to terms with your sin debt, you can be delivered from it. The second step is to repent of your sin, which means to have a change of purpose and direction from sin (2 Corinthians 7:10-11, Acts 2). It is a turning from sin to God to save you. It is a turning from sin to God to transform you. The third step is to accept and to put your trust / confidence in the person of Jesus Christ, who is fully God and fully man and the work of Jesus Christ to save you from the penalty, power, and one day the presence of sin and to set you apart unto a right relationship with God the Father (John 1:12, John 3:1-21, 2Corinthians 7:10-11, Titus 2:11-14, Acts 20:17-21, Acts 17:30-34, Romans 2:1-4).

You rest in the fact and confidence that God's Work on the cross applies to you as you acknowledge your sin condition and your need for His forgiveness, and accept Christ's work as payment for your sin condition. You rest in the fact that you have been saved from the sin condition and position and saved unto a new relationship with God. As we acknowledge that we are sinners and deserve punishment, repent of sin and draw near to put our trust in the literal death, burial, resurrection of Jesus Christ we will be saved from the penalty of sin, the power of sin, and soon the presence sin unto a new and right relationship with God the Father (Ephesians 1:13-14).

Salvation in Jesus Christ changes our position and condition in this world. Through Salvation God puts us in a position whereby we are declared right with God and are at peace with God forever, no longer being His enemy (Romans 5:1-3). This is what we call justification. We are legally declared right in God's sight with no enmity between us any longer. Through Salvation God makes us alive in Jesus Christ resulting in receiving a new position, new power, and a new passion to obey God and to relate with God and to bear fruit for Him (2 Corinthians 5:11-21). This is what we call regeneration. We have been made spiritually alive. Through Salvation, God places us into the family of God forever (Romans 8:15-17). This is what we call adaption. We have been placed into the family of God forever. Being in Jesus Christ changes our lives on earth and in heaven forever.

Sanctification is the Purpose for Salvation

God saved us from the consequences of sin to sanctify us. Sanctification is the end result of being changed into the perfect likeness of Jesus Christ. We were transitioned from sinner to be transformed into a Saint. We were delivered to be developed. God is the one that initiates, maintains, and completes the work of transforming man into the likeness of Jesus Christ for eternity. Therefore, we can rest in the fact that this will be done. Whatever God starts, He finishes. God's complete work of sanctification will end at the return of Jesus Christ. When Christ returns He will make all who are saved in Jesus Christ like Him. We will have a heavenly body to match our heavenly condition and position. In essence sanctification is the carrying on to perfection the work begun in regeneration, which extends to the whole man (Romans 6:13, 2 Corinthians 4:6, Colossians 3:10, 1 John 4:7).

Even though sanctification is the work of God, He involves man in the process. God has set Christians apart to Himself and empowered Christians to participate with Him in the process of making them like Him. God works in Christians and on Christians. As a result he expects Christians to respond to that work through a life of disciplined obedience. In other words, God empowers Christians to participate with Him in the work of sanctification (1John 3:1-3, Romans 8:1-14).

Christians are to be devoted to putting off sin in their lives according to the power of Holy Spirit who works within them (Romans 8:1-14), and are to be devoted to walking in holiness according to the power of the Holy Spirit that works within them. Christians are to spend their lives becoming in practice what they are in position through the power of God within them. Since we are Saints by our position in Jesus Christ , we are to live our lives seeking to be Saints in practice. Since we are set apart to God in position, we are to live our lives being set apart to God in practice. Sanctification is initiated, maintained, and completed by God, but He includes mankind in the process with Him.

God saves and sanctifies mankind for three essential reasons. First, God saves and sanctifies mankind that they may know Him intimately (John 17:1-3). Christians have been saved to have an intimate relationship with God. We were not saved to practice religion. Second, God saves and sanctifies mankind that they may be useful to Him practically (Romans 7:4, Ephesians 2:10). Christians are to be instruments in the Redeemer's Hand. We are called to be useful to God as God carries out His plan on earth. Third, God saves and sanctifies mankind that they may become like Him completely (2 Corinthians 3:18, Romans 8:28-31). Christians have been saved to reflect the very character of God. Our light is to so shine that when men see us, they see the very reflection of God. Therefore, any attempt to live independent of the Creator in thoughts, words, actions, relationship patterns, or lifestyle will result in total devastation for those who reject God's order, design, and will for life (Proverbs 5:21-23).

The Work of the Church the Role of Biblical Counseling

The church must learn how to be a servant of God in His work. Since God is saving souls the church must understand how God wants to use her in that work of salvation. Evangelism must be understood. Evangelism must be developed. Since God is sanctifying souls into His image, the church must understand how God wants to use her in the work of sanctification. Discipleship must be understood and developed. The church cannot honor God if she is not operating as God designed. God chooses to do His work of salvation and sanctification through the church (2 Corinthians 5:18-21, Ephesians 4:11-16). Therefore, a church that is not committed to evangelism and discipleship is a church that is not useful to God in His work of salvation and sanctification. That church is counter-productive.

Counseling must be a by-product of the work of the church as the church learns how to be a servant of God. For example, counseling must function in accordance with the church as the church functions in accordance with God's work of salvation and sanctification. No counseling ministry of church can fulfill the mission of the church if it is does understand and practice evangelism when necessary. Moreover, the counseling ministry of the church cannot fulfill the mission of the church if it does not understand and practice the work of discipleship accordingly. As God saves and sanctifies, we should see the church doing evangelism and discipleship. As the church is doing evangelism and discipleship, we should see her counseling ministry functioning in evangelism and discipleship as well. The counseling ministry should not be a ministry of recovery. Rather, the counseling ministry should be a ministry of repentance and transformation. Counseling cannot honor God if does not operate in correspondence with the work of the Church. Too many churches have embraced a model of counseling that contradicts the work of evangelism and discipleship. There has been an embracing of psychology with a rejection of theology. Counseling has to be in line with evangelism and discipleship, or it cannot be a support of the work of salvation and sanctification.

EVERY CHRISTIAN A COUNSELOR
A FIRM FOUNDATION (PART 2)
CHAPTER 2

Now that we understand the work of God, we can get a clear picture on how the church is to be used of God to accomplish His work. Since God is saving souls from the consequences of sin and sanctifying saints into the likeness of Jesus Christ, everything the church does must correspond to this work of God. God's solution to man's problems is summed up in salvation and sanctification. Man cannot live as God designed without being delivered from sin and being sanctified in Jesus Christ. Every problem of man can be traced back to fall of Adam and the sin consequences that resulted. Therefore, a life lived apart from God is a life that is lived in futility and destined for destruction. As God saves souls from sin and the consequences of sin, and sanctifies man into the likeness of Jesus Christ, He uses the church through the work of evangelism and discipleship to accomplish His work of salvation and sanctification.

The Ministry of Evangelism and It's Outcome

God has given the church the ministry of evangelism (2 Corinthians 5:19-21). In essence, the ministry of evangelism is the responsibility of sharing the good news of the death, burial, resurrection of Jesus Christ and its implications for mankind to the world. The church has the responsibility of making this known to the entire world. This is no small task. As the church does the work of evangelism, God does His work of salvation through their work of evangelism. In other words, as the Body of Christ shares the Gospel of Jesus Christ, God uses that sharing as the avenue to reconcile individuals to Himself. However, we must consider that God reconciles people to Himself accordingly as He wills through that message. It is not automatic that when we share the Gospel people will be saved. It is always in the timing and hand of God.

We cannot ignore the reality that the outcome of the work of evangelism is solely determined by God. We cannot save people from their sin condition. We do not have the power to save people. We have the message that God will use to save people, and we can only provide that message of salvation in a faithful and honest fashion. Too many people get frustrated in sharing their faith because they think it is up to them to save a soul.

On the other hand, too many people don't share their faith because they think is up to them to save a soul and they don't want to fail.

God is the one that will bring people to their senses, grant them repentance and bring them to deliverance from their sin condition through the church's work of evangelism (2 Timothy 2:24-26). We must learn our place in this process. We must be faithful to stay within that place. If not, we may be guilty of irresponsibility or over-responsibility in the work of evangelism.

The Evaluation and Motive of the Work of Evangelism

The work of evangelism should not by evaluated by the outcome of the work but by the church's faithfulness to the work (1 Corinthians 3: 5-9). Some may present the message of the person and work of Jesus Christ to people and see no outcome of salvation. This does not mean that this person has failed. He planted a seed. Others may present the message of the person and work of Jesus Christ to the same people at a later time and see the outcome of salvation with those people. This does not mean that this person has the right method. The person was there at the opportune time as God allotted. The church should not be discouraged if there is no immediate result from the work of evangelism. God is the one that causes the growth. The result of the work is not up to the Body of Christ. The results of evangelism rest completely in the hands of God.

The work of evangelism should flow out of love for others. Since God has called us out of darkness into His marvelous light (Colossians 1:13), we should want others to have that same deliverance out of sin we have gained. There is no fear in love. Therefore, we as Christians must seek the greatest good of the one who needs the gospel, and not be consumed with how they may handle us. Although we know the outcome of salvation is not up to us, the desire for one's salvation should be in us. We must have a desire to see the lost saved. If we do not, we will easily find ourselves banking on the fact that God saves and become complacent in sharing the Gospel, while forgetting the fact that He saves through Christians sharing the Gospel. As a result, the church should be committed to the work of evangelism out of a heart that is concerned about the sin condition of others. Our hearts should be grieved over that fact that there are people in slavery to sin. Christians should be motivated to be a part of the mission to save lost souls as the result of the grief. Love for others should move us to the work of evangelism.

The work of evangelism should not be motivated by seeking to attract a crowd. Evangelism that is based on building numbers for a local church may fall short of God's intent of the message of salvation. The salvation message was not intended to be a marketing tool. It was not designed to build attendance. Evangelism that is based on building numbers for a local church may lean towards reducing people to pawns that fit into an agenda for church growth.

When evangelism is a means to church growth, it no longer serves the purpose for which it is intended. This means the church may possibly be misunderstanding or misguided in the mission God intended. Evangelism that is based on building numbers for a local church can lead to presenting a water-downed version of the message of the person and work of Jesus Christ resulting in peddling a false gospel. A gospel that is used to attract crowds is probably a gospel that is devoid of discussing the reality of sin. People tend not to be attracted to the discussion of sin and condemnation. People tend to be attracted to the discussion of how God or His methods can bring blessing and we must consider the attraction carefully.

The Cross is Offensive to the World

The church must expect people to reject the message of the person and work of Jesus Christ because it is offensive to a sin sick world. The message of the person and work of Jesus Christ is offensive because people tend to think they are basically good. The Gospel is only good news to people who know and understand their depraved and sinful condition. To a person who believes he is okay, that kind of conversation is offensive. The message of the person and work of Jesus Christ is offensive because people tend to minimize the reality of their sin condition and need for restoration from that condition. People tend to compare themselves to others and then determine that they are not that bad. As a result, people are offended when talks about a need to be saved come up because they don't think they are as bad off as others. The message of the person and work of Jesus Christ will be rejected because man in the flesh is hostile towards God and blinded from embracing the message by the devil himself (2 Corinthians 4:1-4). Scripture exposes that man is hostile towards God in the flesh (Romans 8:5-7). Man is under the slavery of the evil one with a harden heart and must be delivered by the power of the Gospel. Therefore, the church must expect rejection of the message understanding the self deception of mankind and the deception of the devil.

Evangelism or Marketing?

The church must not reduce the work of evangelism to marketing. The church must not seek to appeal to the appetites of unbelievers through the work of evangelism. Unbelievers do not have an appetite for God. You can't appeal to their appetites thinking it will lead them to God. The church must not seek to try to make the message of the person and work of Jesus Christ attractive to unbelievers. To make the message attractive is to alter the message. To alter the message is to give a false gospel. The church must not seek to adapt to the world's system in order to draw men. Do not promise people something to attract them only to offer them something different that what you presented. This is called the bait and switch. It is the work of God to draw men and save them and the work of the church to present the message of salvation to them.

Whatever is used to attract people to the church has to be continued to keep them at the church. People who are drawn to the church because of the temporal benefits promoted by that church tend to leave if those benefits cease or if those benefits no longer suit their agenda. For instance, if you promise free daycare so that people would attend your church, you must continue that service for people who come only for the daycare. Once you stop providing free daycare or they no longer have children that age, you may find these people no longer attending the church unless they are captured by the Gospel of Jesus Christ. People who are drawn to a church because of particular personalities promoted by that church tend to leave when those personalities leave or when those personalities no longer suit their agenda. People attract people and people are offended by people. Yet, if those people are not captured by the Gospel of Jesus Christ they will leave or stay according to people and not according to Truth. If Truth is not drawing people to the church, then Truth will not keep people at the church. Remember in John 6 when Jesus challenged people about coming for physical bread instead of coming for eternal bread? We need to be mindful that this still happens today. The work of the Church is not to attract a crowd but to present the message of the person and work of Jesus Christ while God will draw and save souls through that message as He wills not as we work.

The Work of Discipleship

God has given the church the ministry of discipleship. In essence, the ministry of discipleship is teaching believers in Jesus Christ how to walk with Jesus Christ and to become like Him in all aspects of life. The Word of God teaches us how to walk with Jesus Christ. It guides us into all the aspects we need to know to in order walk accordingly. Discipleship involves leading believers from birth in Jesus Christ to being mature in Jesus Christ. This is a process. This process is life-long. Discipleship involves teaching Believers how to love God and love others in a complete systematic way. Loving God requires obedience to what He commands. Loving God requires service to others. In essence, discipleship is the process of helping believers live out in practice what God has made them by position unto maturity in Jesus Christ.

The work of discipleship involves helping believers in Jesus Christ put off patterns of sin in their life. Through the work of discipleship, Believers learn how to lay aside the sinful ways of life they identified with before being saved unto a new life in Jesus Christ. This also called repentance. Repentance is a life-style not an event. Through discipleship believers learn how to make no provision for the sinful tendencies of their flesh that still remains after conversion. This requires setting up road blocks that make it difficult to return to the sinful tendencies through the power of God. This requires learning how to resist sinful tendencies through the power of God. Through discipleship, believers learn how to flee from people, places, and products that can lead them into the former manner of life they had before being saved unto a new life in Jesus Christ. One must come to terms with sin in those areas. Then one can work on fleeing accordingly. Discipleship is the manner by which believers learn how purify themselves from the stains of sin.

The work of discipleship involves helping believers in Jesus Christ put on patterns of righteousness that reflect the character of Jesus Christ. First, Believers in Jesus Christ are taught the standards by which God wants them to live and the importance of living a life that is pleasing to God. Christians evaluate God's standard for thinking, desires, as well as communication. Christians also evaluate God's standards for behavior, relating, and serving. Second, Believers in Jesus Christ learn how to live as Christians in all aspects of life. Christians learn how to carry themselves in a manner that reflects the Jesus Christ in character, conduct, conversation, and even commitments. Third, Christians learn that obedience without the motivation to know God, to become like God, and to be useful to Him is not genuine or beneficial. Obedience without the motivation of pleasing God falls short of its goal. It becomes a religious practice. Through the work of discipleship, Believers in Christ are taught the standards of God and then are trained in walking in the standards of God.

The work of discipleship does not proceed in a regular and unbroken course because Believers in Jesus Christ still sin. Even though Believers in Jesus Christ have been made alive in Christ there are still patterns of sin in their lives that have not been dealt with. This slows the process down. Christians are not sinless, but when we don't deal with sin it creates problems. Patterns of sin create confusion, disorder, and every evil thing in the life of a Believer and others around him or her. This is why we need accountability and support from other Christians. We can't deal with sin by ourselves. Patterns of sin lead Believers to rebel against who they are in Christ and what they have in Christ resulting in being double minded and unstable in all their ways. This explains why some Christians do not look like Christians for certain periods of time. This also explains why we must stay in the habit of confronting sin in the Church. Christians are not sinless but they we do sin less and less as we submit more and more to the work of God. God works on Christians through the church's work of discipleship.

The Objectives of Evangelism and Discipleship

Evangelism and discipleship are the avenue to believing in Christ, to belonging to Jesus Christ, to being useful to Jesus Christ, and to becoming like Jesus Christ. Through evangelism, God reconciles unbelievers to Himself. This reconciliation is to lead to connecting unbelievers who have now become believers to a community of believers who would begin the discipleship process with the new converts. As the church does the work of discipleship, God works through the church to guide people into being useful to Him for good works and to becoming like Him as they learn and apply His Word to their lives. That is what the work of evangelism and discipleship is to be about.

The Use of Spiritual Gifts in the Church

If you are a Christian, you are part of the universal church and should be connected to a local Bible Believing Church. The local church cannot do the work of evangelism and discipleship without the participation of Believers. We were not saved to serve ourselves. We were saved to serve Jesus Christ our Lord. You are a servant! All of us must be committed to our calling. We are the Body of Christ. We are the instruments by which God does His work of salvation and sanctification. As the popular book of Paul Tripp states, we are "Instruments in the Redeemer's Hand." God will use you in the ministry of evangelism and discipleship at that local church through the spiritual gift(s) He has endowed you. Through various gifts given by God to fellow believers, they are able to accomplish God's mission of making disciples of all the nations.

EVERY CHRISTIAN A COUNSELOR
A FIRM FOUNDATION (PART 3)
CHAPTER 3

God is saving souls and maturing saints unto the image of Jesus Christ through the church's work of evangelism and discipleship as each individual of the church functions according to his spiritual gifts within the local assembly. As a result of this, the local church must structure itself in such a manner that can facilitate the work of evangelism and discipleship in a effective, efficient and orderly manner. In the book of Acts we find that the Church functioned in a manner that seemed to be effective, efficient and orderly in relation to the work of evangelism and discipleship. As we evaluate some of the activities of first church in the Book of Acts, we will identify some key principles to consider for organizing and structuring the church for the work of evangelism and discipleship.

The Activities of the First Church

When the first church was established, there are a few key activities the church practiced that we want to consider for our local churches. As we look at these activities, we want to evaluate our churches accordingly. One of the first things we see is that the church baptized individuals who came to faith in the Person and work of Jesus Christ (Acts 2:37-41). I could only imagine what it must have been like to be in a group of three thousand new converts waiting to be baptized!!! I am sure it was an incredible experience. This local Body of Believers also devoted themselves to the teaching of the apostles (Acts 2:42). This was not mere listening. This was a listening to learn so that this local Body of Believers could live according to God's will. Moreover, the church devoted themselves to genuine fellowship with one another (Acts 2:42-44). The connection went beyond shallow hugs and conversation. A genuine joining of lives to build real God-honoring relationships took place. These activities seem to be more than just rote level acts.

In addition to the previous three activities, there were a few other activities that warrant our attention. The church devoted themselves to prayer and praise (Acts 2: 42-47). There was a genuine demonstration of conversation with God. The church showed true thanksgiving to who God is and what He had done. Another activity of the church was that they sold property and possessions to meet the needs of one another when necessary (Acts 2:45). This is the nature of a genuine family. This church was a genuine family. The church even sent missionaries to continue the work that began in Jerusalem (Acts 13: 1-3). They were sensitive to God's calling of missionaries and were obedient to God's call of missionaries. This church was not just a mere group organized for attendance; they were a family connected to love and serve.

Moreover, we can identify two other activities of the first church that we should consider for our churches. The church assigned seven men to the task of overseeing the serving of food to the widows of their congregation so that none would be neglected any longer due to lack of oversight (Acts 6:1-6). They did not overlook problems. They addressed them with proper leadership. Through this we see the activity of organizing the task of serving others for the common good of all that are involved in that local congregation. Organization was needed so that the task could be done properly. This is key to doing ministry in an effective and efficient manner. Through this we also see the activity of establishing leaders to govern the task of serving others for the common good of all that are involved in that local congregation. Ministry does not get organized or accomplished by itself. It takes leaders to organize and to implement ministry with effectiveness and efficiency. The first church gave practical examples for us to follow.

From evaluating the behavior and activities of the first church we get the impression that pursuing to know and love God intimately and loving others practically were the motivations for the activities practiced by the church. These activities were a way a life that demonstrated one was genuinely connected in relationship with God and fellow Believers and not merely religious practices of self righteousness. It did not appear that these individuals were just following orders. It appeared that these individuals were following Jesus Christ. These activities were a demonstration of their love for God and love for others not merely works of service devoid of connection to God and to others. This church demonstrated a faith that works. They also demonstrated a love that labors. This was not fad for this body of Believers. This was a lifestyle—a lifestyle driven by love for God and a lifestyle driven by love for others.

It is through these activities that genuine discipleship and evangelism took place. Devotion to the Apostle's teaching, to prayer, to praising, to baptism, to fellowship, to meeting needs through the selling of possessions and property, to organizing the task of serving others, and to establishing the leaders to govern the task of serving were activities connected to the work of discipleship. These were activities that facilitated spiritual growth directly and in-directly. Sending missionaries to share the Gospel was an activity of the work of evangelism. This initial act of obedience was the catalyst to many churches being started abroad. This initial act of obedience was an act of love. These were not merely programs of the church but activities guided by the cause and effect of love for God and love for others. We were able to see the love working itself out through service. This service was organized and orderly. This service was consistent.

Through the hand of God, these activities of the church resulted in God-honoring results Acts 2:37-47). As a result of their activities, the church was on one accord with each other. Oneness was demonstrated. Unity was demonstrated. As a result of their oneness, the church found favor with all people within their sphere of influence. Their light was shining and reflecting the character of God. So much so that people were drawn in accordingly. God chose to add more people to their community of fellowship. God could trust them with new people. He could trust them because they had proven themselves to be trustworthy. This is something we should consider as we evaluate our churches.

Categorization of the Activities of the First Church

As we evaluate these activities, we can place them into key categories. The activities of baptism and fellowship, can be categorized as the practice of membership (Hebrews 10:23-24, Romans 12:9-10). Membership can be defined as connecting to a local body of believers whereby genuine relationships can be developed. Through these relationships we can develop accountability, spiritual maturity, and godly friendships on a committed and consistent basis. The activity of devotion to the teaching of the Apostles can be categorized as the practice of maturity (Acts 2:42, 2Timothy 4:1-3, Ephesians 4:11-16, Colossians 1:28, Psalm 119:9-11). This is the proper teaching, preaching or studying of the Word. It is done for the purpose of one becoming like Jesus Christ in all aspects of life to a mature man. The activities of prayer and praise can be categorized as the practice of magnification (John 4:21-24). This is the promoting and establishing of an high view of God. It also involves helping individuals understand who God is, how He operates and what God expects of us. Moreover, it involves worshipping God accordingly.

As we continue to evaluate these activities we find three more categories to consider. The activity of selling their possessions and property to the meet the needs of one another accordingly can be categorized as the practice of ministry (Romans 12:3-8, 1Peter 4:10-11, John 13:1-20). That is defined as using our spiritual gifts and talents to bear burdens and to meet needs. It also involves serving others in tangible manners. The activity of sending Paul and Barnabas, to share the Gospel abroad can be categorized as the practice of missions (2Corinthains 5:18-20, Matthew 28:18-20). This is the proper preaching and teaching of the Gospel message. This preaching and teaching is to be taken to the community, the state, the country and the world in order to make Disciples of Jesus Christ. The activities of organizing the task to serve others and establishing leaders to govern the task of serving can be categorized as the practice of management (1 Corinthians 14:40). Management is the practice of directing, organizing, and maintenance of ministries. The purpose of these administrative responsibilities is to keep the ministries operating decently and in order. This is no small task.

Adapting the Categorization to Formalize a Structure for Your Church

If a church is going to be in the position to useful to God in the work of evangelism and discipleship it must consider how to organize and structure itself accordingly. The church needs to establish and organize its activities of love for God and members. This should be done in such a manner that genuine discipleship can take place. The end goal is that spiritual maturity into the image of Christ as God wills would take place. The church needs to establish and organize its activities of love for unbelievers. This should be done in such a manner that genuine evangelism can take place. The end goal would be that salvation would happen for unbelievers as God wills. The church needs faithful leaders and a structure by which all its organized activities of love for God, members, and unbelievers can function accordingly so that genuine evangelism and discipleship can take place resulting in salvation and sanctification as God wills. Through these faithful leaders and structure all the church's organized activities of love for God, members, and unbelievers can function accordingly.

As we have identified the basic activities of the first church and categorized those activities according to six key categories, consider structuring your church through these categories as means of facilitating the work of evangelism and discipleship through your local assembly. Consider structuring your church through 6 key ministry departments of Management, Membership, Magnification, Maturity, Ministry, and Missions. Set it up in such a manner that all ministry activities would be started, organized, and operated by these ministry departments. Any activity or service that does not fit those ministry categories should not be maintained or started. This would keep the church from spending time and resources on a ministry that does not need to be maintained or started. As each department of ministry and the individual ministries under each department functions according to the categories described, the work of evangelism and discipleship can take place in an effective, efficient and orderly manner.

As we have identified how the first church established leaders to govern the ministry activities, consider establishing leaders to govern all the ministries and all the ministry departments established. Directors should be established to oversee, manage, and direct individual ministries under each ministry department. Also, coordinators should be established to oversee, manage and direct individual ministries under each ministry department. In addition, team leaders should be established to oversee, manage and direct individual ministries under each ministry department. Deacons should be established to manage, oversee, and direct the ministry departments. Directors should also be considered to manage, oversee and direct the ministry departments. The directors can serve under the deacons accordingly. Pastor-teaches

24

would be involved in the counsel and equipping of all members accordingly. They would be involved in the preaching and teaching of the members. They would be involved in the training of saints for sanctification and service accordingly. As leaders are established according to the need of each department of ministry, the work of evangelism and discipleship can take place in an effective, efficient, and orderly manner.

An Example of How it Could Work

As each department of ministry and the individual ministries under each department functions according to the categories described, let us consider how each department of ministry can work together to facilitate the work of evangelism and discipleship. The Ministry of Missions becomes the avenue by which the local congregation trains every individual within the local assembly in the fundamentals of sharing and defending the Gospel of Jesus Christ. This would also include facilitating all efforts within the local congregation of sharing the good news. This task would take a lot of organization and structure. All local efforts and activities of the congregation to share the good news would be approved, established, organized and governed by the Ministry of Missions as allowed by the overseer(s)of the entire church. This would be in relation to formalized activities where groups are representing the local body and needing resources of the local body accordingly. This would not be in relation to personal evangelistic efforts. All national and international efforts and activities of the congregation to share the good news would be approved, established, organized and governed by the Ministry of Missions as allowed by the overseer(s) of the entire church. This too would be in relation to formalized activities where groups are representing the local body and are in need of resources from that body. This would not be in relation to personal efforts. The Ministry of Missions would become the central means by which all training and organized efforts of the congregation to share the gospel would be governed.

As individuals place their faith in the finished work of Jesus Christ through the Ministry of Missions, the work of the Ministry of Membership would begin its part. All efforts and activities to connect new converts and existing members of the church to each other for genuine fellowship, relationships, and accountability between one another would be approved, started, established, organized and governed by the Ministry of Membership as allowed by the overseer(s) of the entire church. This is where formalized small groups and would be formed. The Ministry of Membership would make sure that every new convert and existing members in the local assembly are not left alone or disconnected from the local assembly through organized checks and balances established, organized, facilitated, and governed by the ministry.

The Ministry of Maturity would begin its work as the Ministry of Memberships connects each individual to small groups within the local assembly. The Ministry of Maturity would become the avenue by which the spiritual development and growth of all into the likeness of Christ in all aspects of life within the congregation would be established, organized, facilitated and governed as allowed by the overseer(s) of the entire church. This is essential. A church that does not develop in maturity will have a community of babes. There has to be people within the ministry who understand the process of change in order to have something like this process in place. This would include people who know how to find, develop, and use good curriculum. Putting together a system of this magnitude requires a lot of cooperation on behalf of the leaders and the congregation. A system of this magnitude would require faithful participation at all levels. Imagine the possibilities.

As the Ministry of Maturity is facilitating the spiritual development of the congregation, the Ministry of Magnification would be facilitating the gathering together of all within the local assembly for corporate worship and prayer. The Ministry of Magnification would establish, organize, facilitate, and govern the implementation of all aspects worship and prayer of the Sunday Morning Worship services, communion activities, baptisms, testimonial services, and corporate prayer times as allowed by the overseer(s) of the entire church. This ministry would be the keepers and coordinators of all such matters. The keepers and coordinators of this ministry would need to be mature in genuine praise and worship so that they would be a model for others. This kind of service is more than picking praise music and establishing a prayer time. A ministry of this caliber is seeking to prepare and promote the genuine worship and praise of God, not just publically but also privately.

As the Ministry of Magnification is facilitating corporate genuine worship of God, the Department of Ministry would take responsibility for making sure each individual within the local church has been served according to their issues or concerns. The Department of Ministry would facilitate the establishing, organizing, and governing of all activities within the local assembly that bare the burdens and meet the needs of individuals within the local assembly as allowed by the overseer(s) of the entire church. The tangible needs of individuals within the local assembly would be addressed through this ministry. People in need of money or possessions within reason would find support through this ministry. The Department of Ministry would establish, organize, and govern a system of training all individuals within the local assembly in the doctrine of spiritual gifts. As result of teaching individuals the doctrine of spiritual gifts, the ministry would help individuals connect with ministry activities whereby they can serve according to their spiritual gifts. The ministry would help them connect with a ministry activity in accordance to their spiritual gifts. If the ministry is developed properly, the majority of the members would be serving accordingly resulting in needs being met accordingly.

The Ministry of Management would be the ministry by which all other ministries would receive their administrative support to function. The Ministry of Management would provide all the financial, organizational, and maintenance support necessary for all ministry activities within the local assemblies. This ministry would be foundational for all other ministries. This ministry would handle all the issues pertaining to the practical matters of functioning. The ministry would handle matters such as paying the monthly bills of lights, gas, phone, mortgage or insurance payments. The ministry would also handle matters such as cleaning the building, setting up chairs and rooms, computers, or workstations that provide staples, printers, copy machines. The Ministry of Management would deal with any and all legal and organizational matters and would guard the church from lawsuits, making sure that the church is following the laws of the land. The ministry would seek to make sure that all activities of the church are functioning within the guidelines set by the overseers of the church.

The Benefits to Consider

When ministries are organized and structured into categories, it brings definition and clarification to the work of the ministry. Definition and clarification of ministry will help in establishing the purpose and mission of each ministry activity. The purpose and mission declares why a ministry exist. It sets the direction for the ministry. Establishing the purpose and mission of each ministry activity will help in establishing the objectives of each ministry activity. The objectives give over arching goals to the ministry. These goals are what the ministry is always trying to accomplish. Moreover, establishing the objectives of each ministry activity will help in establishing the process of operation for each ministry activity. The process gives procedure to the accomplishing of the purpose and mission. The process gives procedure to the objectives which will accomplish the purpose and mission. As we have been called to the work of evangelism and discipleship let us consider developing leadership and organizing and structuring our ministries both present and future according to categories mentioned in this chapter with intent of facilitating the work of evangelism and discipleship though these departments of ministries.

Every Christian a Counselor
A Firm Foundation (Part 4)
Chapter 4

So far we have come to discover that God is saving souls and maturing saints unto the image of Jesus Christ through the church's work of evangelism and discipleship as each individual of the church functions according to his spiritual gifts within the local assembly. As a result of this, the local church must develop leadership and structure itself in such a manner that it can facilitate the work of evangelism and discipleship in an effective, efficient and orderly manner. We suggested the categories of Missions, Membership, Maturity, Magnification, Ministry, and Management as a structure along with developing team leaders, directors, deacons, and pastor-teachers as a leadership structure to govern these areas so that the work of evangelism and discipleship can be done in a effective, efficient and orderly manner. If you are thinking, "what does all this have to do with biblical counseling," the answer is: everything. Steve Viars says *"You can't have an effective counseling ministry until you have a ministry that counsels." In other words, a church that is not functioning effectively, efficiently, and orderly in the work of evangelism and discipleship cannot have a counseling ministry that functions as God intended.* Therefore, we must understand and develop a church that counsels via evangelism and discipleship before we can have an effective counseling ministry. As God is saving souls and maturing saints into the image of Jesus Christ through the work of evangelism and discipleship, we must understand the phases of change, the stages of spiritual growth, areas where change is to take place. We must also seek to understand how the Word of God is used in connection with this insight in the work of evangelism and discipleship.

The Phases of Change

In order for an individual to have the salvation-sanctification experience through the work of evangelism and discipleship there are phases that must take place in his life. In order for the salvation-sanctification experience to take place in the life of an individual through the work of evangelism and discipleship there must be a point of *realization* (2 Timothy 2:24-26). Realization is the awareness of truth. One sees he is either out of fellowship with God or has no relationship with God resulting in understanding the truth about God, self, others, and circumstances. Realization must move into *remorse* (2 Corinthians 7:10). Remorse is the conviction and godly sorrow over sin. There is recognition and godly sorrow over sin in lifestyle, sin against God, and sin with or against people. Along with this recognition is a desire to make things right with God and others as needed. Remorse must move into *renouncement* (Psalm 32:1-11). Renouncement is the agreement and acknowledgement to God that one has sinned. It is an acknowledgement of sin against God, others, or in lifestyle. It is accompanied with a desire to turn from that sin in lifestyle against God and others.

As remorse must move to renouncement, renouncement must move to *repentance* (2 Corinthians 7:10-11, Proverbs 28:13). Repentance is the practice of putting off the sinful patterns of life against God and with others accordingly. Repentance must move to *renewing* (Ephesians 4:17-23). Renewing is the process of developing one's mind in the truth of God's Word. It comes through meditating on God's Word. It includes studying the Word of God so that one may know what and how to obey God and to love others accordingly. Renewing must move to *replacement* (Ephesians 4:17-32). Replacement is the putting on the new way of life in Jesus Christ. This includes training in functioning as Jesus Christ would in all aspects of life accordingly. This is a process not an event.

The Work of God, the Work of Ministry and the Word of God in the Phases of Change

These six phases—realization, remorse, renouncement, repentance, renewal, and replacement—can only happen with an individual through the work of God not the will of man. God must provide recognition in order for one to realize (2 Timothy 2:24-26). No one can break through the walls of deception without God. God has to bring the awareness. God must produce regret from within in order for one to remorse and renounce (2 Corinthians 7:10-11). No one comes to Jesus Christ without Jesus Christ (John 6:1-71).

Salvation is a gift of God not by works so that no man can boast (Ephesians 2:1-10). God must regenerate in order for one to realize, remorse, renounce, repent, renew, and replace. You must be born again to be able to live a life of realization, renouncing, remorse, repenting, renewing and replacing (Titus 2: 11-15). Salvation is not the end but the beginning of your life with God. As you are made alive you have ability to realize, remorse, renounce, repent, renew and replace through the power of God within (Philippians 2:12-16).

The work of evangelism and discipleship is done by guiding individuals to and through these six phases as each ministry does their part corporately as empowered by God do so. The Missions and Magnification Ministry would be used to guide individuals to and through four key phases. Mission and Magnification would be used to guild individuals through the phases of realization, remorse, renouncement and repentance. This is done as God wills not as we work. The Departments of Membership, Maturity, and Ministry would be used to guide individuals to and through the three key phases of repentance, renewal, and replacement as God wills. This also is done as God wills not as we work. The Management Ministry would make sure all ministries are running properly to facilitate the process. Leaders from each area would be networking the assimilation of individuals accordingly. All the administrative duties that are necessary to carry out these various tasks would be implemented accordingly. This would be done decently and in order anticipating the salvation of sinners and the sanctification of saints as God wills.

The work of evangelism and discipleship is done by guiding individuals to and through the six phases as each individual uses their spiritual gift(s) accordingly within the six key ministries indentified in the previous paragraph as empowered by God do so. Individuals would use their gifts within the six key ministries organized to proclaim, teach, and defend the Gospel, and other key components of the Word of God.

Through this work, they may move individuals to and through these phases as God wills. Individuals can focus on faithfulness while trusting God with the results. Individual would use their gifts within the six key ministries organized to bare burdens, and meet needs. Through this work, they may move individuals to and through the six phases as God wills. This brings clarity and proper expectation to the ones serving through their gifts. This work is to be a labor of love for God and others.

The work of evangelism and discipleship is done by guiding individuals to and through the six phases as each ministry and individual uses the Word of God accordingly (2 Timothy 3:16-17). The Word of God was intended to be used for teaching the truth according to the need of the moment. This kind of teaching would not be random facts of the Bible. This would be teaching that is relevant to their situation before God and others. The Word of God was intended to be used for reproof. Reproof is conviction about a matter in one's life that needs to be changed. One is convicted of sin and recognizes something needs to be down about it. The Word of God was intended to be used for correction and training in righteousness. Correction is showing individuals how to turn from what is wrong according to Scripture. Training in righteousness is to show individuals how to walk habitually in what is right according to Scripture. This work results in leading an individual to maturity in Christ and being equipped for every good work in Christ.

The Stages of Spiritual Growth and the Work of Evangelism and Discipleship

The way in which the Word of God is to be used unfolds the stages by which we grow in spiritual maturity into the likeness of Jesus Christ. First, the Word of God is profitable for teaching. The first stage of spiritual growth is the *teaching stage*. The teaching stage is the stage in which one comes to know and understand the truth of

God's Word in relation to God, self, others, or situation in order to grow into spiritual maturity in Christ. Second, the Word of God is profitable for reproof. This leads to the second stage of spiritual growth which is the *conviction stage*. The conviction stage is the stage in which individuals come to see that they are in sin in relation to God, others, or situation according to the standards of the Word of God. Third, the Word of God is profitable for correction. This leads to the third stage of spiritual growth which is the *correction stage*. The correction stage is the stage in which one is learning and progressing in turning from what is wrong in his relationship with God, self and others. Fourth, the Word of God is profitable for training in righteousness. This leads to the fourth stage of spiritual growth which is the *training stage*. The training stage is the stage in which one is learning and progressing in walking in what is right to maturity in Christ as directed by the Word of God.

Knowing the phases of change and the stages of spiritual growth will help us to understand how to use the Word of God accordingly for the work of Evangelism and Discipleship. For instance, if a person is lacking realization they need to be taken to and through the teaching stage, they need to come to recognize the Truth. They need to understand and know the Truth of the Word of God as God wills. If a person has realization but is lacking remorse they need to be taken to and through the conviction stage. They need to come to a place of regret leading to remorse about their sins. This remorse should lead to the Gospel message being presented and the regeneration (salvation) of individuals by God as He wills, resulting in renouncing and repenting of their sin unto salvation for the unbeliever. If a person is remorseful and has renounced and repented unto salvation he needs to be taken to and through the correction stage. In the correction stage he would renounce and repent of sin that is hindering fellowship and spiritual maturity in Christ Jesus as God wills. If there has been renouncing and repenting of sin, he needs to be taken to and through the training stage. In the training stage he would renew his mind with truth for right living and replace sin with right living as God wills.

Areas of Life Where Change Is to Take Place

As we help individuals through the phases of change, and the stages of spiritual growth through the work of evangelism and discipleship, there are key areas of life where this change has to take place. Change has to take place in the areas of thoughts, attitudes, desires, and intentions (2 Corinthians 10:3-6, Romans 12:2, Colossians 3:1-7, 1 Corinthians 4:5). The choices we make in life stem from these areas. Change also has to take place in the areas of conversation and lifestyle (Ephesians 4:17-29).

We should not proclaim our new position in Jesus Christ while continuing to willfully practice our old manner of conversation and lifestyle of sin. Moreover, change has to take place in the areas of serving and relating to others (Romans 12:3-21). People should see the character of Christ as they watch how we serve and relate to others. These areas of life are central to all that we experience in life. When there are problems in our lives we can trace them back to problems of sin in these areas. Can you think of one problem in your life that does not include at least one the areas mentioned above? Without understanding this we may fall short in our work of evangelism and discipleship.

These areas of life are key, and change has to take place in them for two central reasons. These are the areas of life where God holds man accountable to obey Him. When you evaluate Scripture, you will find that when we are called to change, it comes back to thoughts, attitudes, desires, intention, conversation, lifestyle, serving, and relational patterns. It cannot be ignored if real change is going to take place. No one else can be responsible to obedience or for disobedience of an individual in these areas of life. People may have had influence in these areas but man controls choice in these areas (Galatians 6:7-8). Therefore no one can blame anyone for the choices they have made in these areas.

Man has to be delivered from his sin condition by God in order to obey God in these key areas of life. This is why man needs to hear and embrace the Gospel of Jesus Christ. If man were able to excuse himself of his choices because of the influence of others, he would not have to stand accountable for sin before God (2 Corinthians 5: 9-10). If man were able to excuse himself his choices because of the influence others, he would not need the Gospel of Jesus Christ.

The Work of Evangelism

We must help individuals through the phases of change and the stages of spiritual growth in relation to the key areas of life where change has to happen. In order to do this, we need to do the work of evangelism properly before transitioning into the work of discipleship. We need to present the Gospel message in a clear and concise manner. In order to do this we must be clear in our understanding of the Gospel message. We don't want to present a faulty message where we present a works oriented gospel or man centered gospel. Second, we need to make sure our hearers understood our message. Asking for feedback is important. We want to evaluate to see if they were able to comprehend the message presented. Finally, we need not be afraid to talk about sin. The gospel is only good news to sinners. If one is not a sinner he does not need the gospel. Therefore, you cannot talk about the Gospel without dealing with the issue of sin.

Knowing our message and knowing the God of our message should have a profound impact on our commitment to show care and concern through the work of evangelism. We need to meet legitimate, tangible needs of unbelievers unconditionally and use it as platform to share the Gospel of Jesus Christ. Meeting legitimate tangible needs of unbelievers is not the Gospel! It is the avenue we should use to share the Gospel. We need to speak up for injustice and use it as a platform to share the Gospel of Jesus Christ. Speaking up for injustice is not the Gospel! It is the avenue we use to share the Gospel. We need to lovingly challenge people in our assembly who profess to

33

be Christians but in actuality are not with the Gospel of Jesus Christ. There must be a constant challenging of the members of the church with the Gospel of Jesus Christ. Some have heard but have not embraced the message.

The Work of Discipleship

As the work of evangelism transitions into the work of the discipleship, knowing the phases of change, the stages of spiritual growth, and the key areas where change takes place, can help the church to construct a system of discipleship that can lead one to spiritual maturity in Christ as God wills. To lead people from spiritual birth to spiritual maturity, the church must coordinate a system of discipleship by which all in the local assembly learn the essential doctrines of the Christian faith. This can be done through class room or home group training. This can be done though sound biblically based curriculum. The essential doctrines consist of things such as the doctrine of God, Man, Jesus Christ, Sin, Salvation, Holy Spirit, Last things, Angels, Demons, Spiritual Leadership, Spiritual Gifts, Sanctification, Old Testament, New Testament, Stewardship, Bema Judgment, White Throne Judgment, and Rewards in Heaven must be taught to the entire congregation. These doctrines are essential to understanding and living the Christian faith. Therefore, the church must be proactive and creative in how this insight is provided to the body. This will require prayer, research and a lot of leg work. In addition to learning the essential doctrines of the faith, the church must coordinate a system of discipleship by which all in the local assembly learn and practice the essential disciplines of the Christian faith. The essential disciplines of the Christian faith consist of things such as confessing of sin, repenting of sin, meditating on the Word of God, forgiving others, applying truth to all aspects of life, serving others according to your spiritual gifts, praying, and worshipping. These are the avenues to knowing, becoming, and being useful to Jesus Christ which means these disciplines are to be practiced not just learned.

Moreover, the church must coordinate a system of discipleship by which all in the local assembly learn and practice the essential duties of the Christian faith. The essential duties of the Christian faith consist of things such as bearing burdens, meeting needs, proclaiming the Gospel of Jesus Christ, defending the Gospel of Jesus Christ, giving monetarily to support the work of the local assembly, corporate worship and corporate prayer. Learning and living these duties will get individuals within the local assembly connected to serving one another. These essential duties are vital to building relationships that reflect the character of our Lord God, and Savior Jesus Christ. Furthermore, the church must coordinate a system of discipleship by which all in the local assembly learn how function in a God-honoring way within the essential demographics they are in. For instance, we want people to learn how to be godly parents, husbands, wives, men, women, teenagers, singles, widows, college students, senior citizens, or young adults. This gets into to the day to day practice of living for

34

Christ within the context one is in. Living properly in you demographic brings glory to God.

The system of discipleship can be developed either in centralized or decentralized ways. Centralized systems would consist of formal classes that are structured and organized at the church location according to doctrines, disciplines, duties, and demographics. It would require built-in applications that require the students to review and work through the material with the intent to live it and not just learn it. It would also require individuals to apply the material within accountability groups that promote doing of the information learned. Decentralized systems would consist of small groups or one on one gatherings whereby individuals are assigned to certain people or small groups that take the responsibility of walking the individuals through the knowledge and practice of the doctrines, disciplines, duties, and demographics on a more informal basis away from the church and in settings such as their home, jobs, coffee houses, etc. Whatever system is chosen, the goal is to make sure that each individual in the local assembly is being trained to know and live by the essential doctrines, disciplines, duties, and demographics to glory of God and growth of the Body of Christ.

Interpersonal Relationships and the Work of Evangelism and Discipleship

As we embrace the work of evangelism and discipleship with all the intricate details mentioned above, we must remember that it is through interpersonal relationships that this work is done. As we develop interpersonal relationships with unbelievers we must consider that we are ambassadors with the primary objective of presenting the gospel. This does not mean that we do not spend time having fun with these individuals. It means that our ultimate agenda is that we present the gospel message. As we develop interpersonal relationships with Christians, we must consider that we are builders with the primary objective of helping believers become like Christ in all aspects to spiritual maturity. We do many things with other Christians. We need to make sure that we do not forget the main thing of helping them grow in spiritual maturity in Jesus Christ our Lord.

Our relationships must be governed by these primary objectives if the work of evangelism and discipleship is to be a way of life and not some religious activity void of love for God and love for others. The Church must consider all these factors before considering developing a biblical counseling ministry. If they have these things in place they will see that a biblical counseling ministry is not hard to implement.

EVERY CHRISTIAN A COUNSELOR
CHAPTER 5
A DEFINITION OF BIBLICAL COUNSELING

As we develop a church that is committed, organized, and structured around evangelism and discipleship, we can have an effective counseling ministry. Since the work of evangelism and discipleship with all the intricate details mentioned is done effectively and efficiently through interpersonal relationships, we must build our relationships with that in mind. As we develop interpersonal relationships, we must consider that we are ambassadors to unbelievers with the primary objective of presenting the gospel to unbelievers. We must also consider that we are builders with believers with the primary objective of helping believers become like Christ in all aspects to spiritual maturity.

If sin is not man's problem then the person and work of Jesus of Christ is not the solution. We know from Scripture that sin is man's essential problem of life. God's solution to man's problem of sin is summed up in the work of salvation and sanctification. God does the work of salvation and sanctification through using the church through work of evangelism and discipleship.

Biblical counseling is the work of evangelism and discipleship on a one on one basis starting with identifying the problem and using the Word of God to work through the solution of salvation or sanctification according to the need of the moment as God wills. Therefore, genuine biblical counseling is an avenue whereby evangelism and discipleship takes place on an interpersonal level. The Word of God is used within the context it was written to address the problems and concerns of individuals anticipating the salvation of sinners and the sanctification of Saints as God wills. Every Christian is called to the work of evangelism and discipleship, which means every Christian is called to the work of biblical counseling. At some level all of us have had to address some problem or concern on an interpersonal level with someone which lead to using the Word of God to either lead them to Christ or to help them change and grow in Christ. As we have examined the work of God, and the work of the church, let us now examine the definition and role of biblical counseling in the local church.

The Definition of Biblical Counseling

Before we can understand how to implement the ministry of biblical counseling we must give a clear definition of biblical counseling. Biblical counseling can be defined as using the Word of God (the Bible) within the context it was written to provide solutions and the application of those solutions to non organic, immaterial, spiritual, and what the world calls "psychological" or "mental disorder" problems. The Word of God is used in a precise and efficient manner to address these matters. The Word of God is used anticipating the salvation of sinners and the sanctification of Saints as a result. Biblical counseling can also be defined as using the Word of God to give comprehensive answers to non-physical problems on a small group level or one on one interpersonal level. In essence, biblical counseling is applied biblical systematic theology. It is the practical ministry that comes out of knowing and understanding the Bible and the theology of the Bible. Biblical Counseling is the practical, comprehensive ministry of soul care that comes out of knowing, understanding, and applying biblical systematic theology to life issues.

The Objectives of Biblical Counseling and The Means By Which they are Accomplished

Biblical counseling has three key objectives. First, biblical counseling seeks to lead a person into salvation when it is discovered that the individual is not a Christian. Biblical counseling does not assume one is a Christian. It seeks to evaluate where one is, and when the time is right, it provides one with the Gospel of Jesus Christ. Second, biblical counseling seeks to help Christians put off sinful patterns of relating and living. Counselors learn the areas where problems exist. Through wise counsel of the Word of God they lead individuals into proper avenues of turning away from sin in those areas. Third, Biblical counseling seeks to help Christians put on godly patterns of relating and living. As the counselor helps individuals put off their sin, they teach them how to walk in what is right according to the Word of God. The counselor shows them how to love God and love others accordingly.

Biblical counseling seeks to accomplish its objectives by seeking to lead people into gaining understanding in three essential categories of life through the Word of God within the context it was written and within the context of their situation. First, through the Word of God, biblical counseling seeks to lead people into gaining a godly perspective of God within the context of their situation. The wrong perspective of God leads to the wrong conclusions of life resulting in living a lack faith which is sin. Second, through the Word of God, biblical counseling seeks to lead people into gaining a godly perspective of themselves, and others within the context of their situation. Pride leads people to see themselves and others according to their opinions and the opinions of others. As a result, one lacks and needs a biblical perspective of themselves and others. Third, through the Word of God, biblical counseling seeks to lead people into gaining a godly perspective of their situation. Individuals seek to evaluate their lives according to their feelings. Biblical counseling seeks to help people interpret life by Truth so that they may live as God commands in their situations.

Biblical counseling seeks to accomplish its objectives by using the Word of God within the context it was written to help people address the issues of life where God holds man accountable to obedience and for disobedience.(See James 3:13-4:10, Luke 6:43-45, Matthew 6:19-21, and Ezekiel 14:1-11) First, biblical counseling uses the Word of God to help people deal with the thoughts, attitudes, and intentions of the heart where God holds mankind accountable to obedience and for disobedience. Second, biblical counseling uses the Word of God to help people deal with the desires of the heart accordingly. Third, biblical counseling Biblical counseling uses the Word of God to help people deal with communicational, behavioral, and relational patterns that God holds mankind accountable to obedience and for disobedience.

In dealing with thoughts, attitudes, motives, desires, communicational patterns, behavioral patterns, and relational patterns where God holds man accountable to obedience and for disobedience, the Word of God is used within the context it was written to guide people into the put-off-put-on process. (See Colossians 3:5-9, Ephesians 4:17-22, 1John 1:9, Proverbs 28:13-14) On a one on one interpersonal level, or on a small group level, biblical counseling takes the Word of God to help people come to the realization of the Truth and genuine remorse over the consequences of sin. There can be no change without realization. In the same manner, biblical counseling takes the Word of God to help people come to genuine renouncement of their sin. If you don't acknowledge your sin you can't deal with your sin. Moreover, biblical counseling takes the Word of God to help people come to genuine repentance of their sin. There can be no transformation without turning from sin. In addition, biblical counseling takes the Word of God to help people renew their minds in the right way of living. Right thinking leads to a right lifestyle. Finally biblical counseling takes the Word of God and help people replace their former manner of life with the new way of living in Jesus Christ our Lord. In essence, biblical counseling addresses the problems presented and the problems discovered in counseling and leads individuals to find their solutions through the Word of God, anticipating salvation for the sinner and progressive sanctification for the Saint. In those areas of the heart where man is not held accountable to obedience and for disobedience such as experiencing joy or sorrow, or experiencing pleasure and pain, counselors weep those who weep, and rejoice with those who rejoice.

Moral Issues and Non-Moral Issues and Counseling

When it comes to moral issues, spiritual matters, immaterial heart issues, or what the world calls "psychological" or "mental disorders," Christians are warned not to engage in or adhere to the counsel of unbelievers. In Psalm 1, Christians are told they are blessed if they do not partake of the counsel of the ungodly. When it comes to problems that are non-physical and moral we are called to stay away from counsel that is not of God. It won't lead us in the direction necessary for genuine change. In Colossians 2:8 Christians are warned not to be indoctrinated by the philosophies of the ungodly but to stand strong in the doctrines taught by Jesus Christ. The world's system requires you to function the world's way. Therefore, if you listen to the world you can't listen to God. In Romans 12:2, Christians are told not to be conformed to this world but to be transformed through the renewing of the mind (in Scripture) which would lead to understanding the will of God. We must direct ourselves according to God's standard. Non-physical moral matters require the wisdom of the Word of God.

However, when it comes to issues that are non-moral or matters of preference, Christians are free to listen to suggestions or gather data from various resources apart from the Word of God. Non-moral issues such as plumbing, car repair, remodeling, TV repair, decorating, gardening, golfing, sports or matters likes these are matters where God allows Christians to have their own standard before Him (Romans 14). Christians are open to listen to suggestions, or to gather data from various resources apart from the Word of God on non-moral issues such as those mentioned above. They are allowed to listen to other resources on matters such as these because the Word of God does not address these matters in specifics. These issues are not necessarily connected to developing or sustaining spiritual life itself. They can be a hindrance to spiritual growth in Christ when they become our preoccupation of life (1John 2:14-15, Hebrews 12:1-2). One's spiritual development is not determined by them. Yet, one's spiritual development can be hindered by them (1Corinthians 6:12).

On the other hand, when it comes to moral issues, spiritual matters, immaterial heart issues, or what the world calls "psychological" or "mental disorders," Christians are to receive their counsel and their insight from counselors who use the Word of God and do not integrate psychological principles or human wisdom with the Word of God. When it comes to the proper ways of how to think or desire, Christians are to gain their insight from counselors who use the Word of God and do not integrate psychological principles or human wisdom with the Word of God. The wisdom of the world cannot lead us to the transformation of God. Therefore, it is useless when it comes to knowing and living the will of God. When it comes to the proper ways of how to speak, live, or behave, Christians are to gain their insight from counselors who use the Word of God and do not integrate psychological principles or human wisdom with the Word of God.

The world can't teach you how to live in a manner that is pleasing to God. Therefore, to mix the wisdom of the world with God's wisdom is confusing and futile. When it comes to the proper ways of how to relate or serve others, Christians are to gain their insight from counselors who use the Word of God and do not integrate psychological principles or human wisdom with the Word of God. The Word of God has so much to teach us about relationships. We would be wise to listen.

The Evaluation of Biblical Counseling

Biblical Counseling can be evaluated from three different areas. We can evaluate biblical counseling from a *conceptual* perspective. That involves evaluating various biblical concepts, insights and principles that are taught to accomplish the objectives of biblical counseling.

We can also evaluate biblical counseling from a *methodological* perspective. This involves looking at various biblical models of counseling. These models are evaluated to see the different biblical techniques that are used in the practice of biblical counseling to help accomplish the objectives of biblical counseling.

Moreover, we can evaluate biblical counseling from an *apologetical* perspective. This involves looking at various logical and theological ways we can defend the work of biblical counseling in relation to secular models and integrated models of counseling.

The conceptual perspective of biblical counseling determines what Truth is to be presented in biblical counseling. The conceptual perspective of biblical counseling defines, explains and interprets the problems presented by the counselee from a biblical perspective. If you do not understand how to interpret the problems that people bring to counseling, you cannot provide the proper solutions in counseling. The concepts, insights, and principles of the Bible clearly define, explain and interpret life's problems in such a manner that we are able to see that even though the world comes up with new categories of problems, there is nothing new under the sun or the Son. Moreover, the conceptual perspective of biblical counseling identifies the solutions and goals to accomplish in biblical counseling. What good is it to know what is wrong from a biblical perspective but not be able to give proper solutions? As we define the specific problems from Scripture, we can determine the specific solutions from Scripture which form the various concepts, insights, and principles we present in the counseling sessions. As the problems, solutions, and goals are defined biblically, the counselor can determine and distinguish between the root sins and fruit sins and help counselees move in the right direction as determined by the Scriptures.

The methodological perspective determines how the truth is to be presented and how the counselee is to be approached in the work of biblical counseling. The methodological perspective of biblical counseling determines the model of biblical counseling. In evaluating biblical counseling from a methodological perspective, we indentify different ways one is to approach various sin matters using the Word of God. There is an evaluation of how one is to lead an individual into the process of biblical change using the Word of God. The methodological perspective also determines the structure of biblical counseling sessions. This involves learning the steps one is to take in a session and when to take those steps. The methodological perspective also determines the process of biblical counseling sessions. This involves learning how to gather data from a counselee or when to console and confront a counselee accordingly.

The apologetical perspectives of biblical counseling reveal how we defend the work of biblical counseling to all who question the validity of it. The apologetical perspective of biblical counseling determines how we defend the legitimacy of biblical counseling in comparison to psychological counseling. This involves understanding and developing a biblical worldview by which one is able to explain biblical counseling in comparison to psychology. It also involves evaluating the worldview of psychology in contrast to biblical counseling in order to challenge the validity of psychology in comparison to biblical counseling. The apologetical perspective of biblical counseling determines how we defend the legitimacy of biblical counseling in comparison to counseling that integrates the Bible with psychological principles. This involves showing the superiority of God's wisdom to man's wisdom. This perspective also involves showing the futility of mixing God's wisdom with man's wisdom in the context of counseling. Consequently, the apologetical perspective gives light as to how we defend the legitimacy of biblical counseling to the Body of Christ. This involves helping Christians embrace the sufficiency of Scripture to deal with all man's moral non-organic, non-physical, mental, or psychological problems.

Biblical Counseling and Worldviews

Your perspective and practice of counseling will be determined by your worldview. The more biblical your worldview, the more biblical your perspective and practice of counseling will be. The less biblical your worldview, the less biblical your perspective and practice of counseling will be. Your worldview is determined by the people you allow to teach you. These people will determine how biblical or unbiblical your perspective and practice of counseling will be. The teachers you allow to instruct you shape your perspective, values, and goals of life. If you want to know who is shaping your concept of counseling, there are three basic questions you can ask. The first question you would ask is what do you define or explain as the nature of man? Every counseling system has a view of man which determines how they approach man. The second question you would ask is what do you believe is wrong with man? This will help you to see if your belief of the problem is sin based or some other idea born out of the wisdom this world's system. The third question you would ask is what do you believe is the solution to man's problem? This will help you see if the wisdom of world or the wisdom of God is predominately guiding your methodology. These questions help you to evaluate if you are influenced by biblical theology or humanistic psychology in your view of counseling. If one does not see biblical counseling as an outworking of evangelism and discipleship on an interpersonal or small group level they will buy into secular models that seek to help people "feel better" instead buying into models that help people "become better." In other words, the focus of counseling will be self-centered instead of God-centered.

The Premise of all Models of Biblical Counseling

In all the various models of biblical counseling the basic premise is still the same. The basic premise is to help individuals know Christ, be useful to Christ, and to become like Christ. This is done through various ways of helping people put off sin and put on righteousness through the power of God. The Word of God will be used to expose truth to individuals about God, self, others, and circumstances. Moreover, the Word of God will be the foundation to all discussion, interpretations, and solutions. Because the Word of God is superior to human wisdom, there will be no mixing of the wisdom of man to address the moral non-organic, heart issues, spiritual matters, or what the world calls "psychological" or "mental disorders." In addition, there will be division between root issues and the fruit issues in relation to the matters being addressed. Assignments will be given to help individuals learn, grow, and change to be like Christ in all aspects of life. All true biblical counseling is the work of discipleship starting with the problem and walking through the work of evangelism and discipleship accordingly. As a result, we see the salvation-sanctification experience take place as God wills. If you don't see these elements, you must question the kind of counseling that is taking place.

EVERY CHRISTIAN A COUNSELOR
CHAPTER 6
KEY MECHANICS OF BIBLICAL COUNSELING

Now that we have come to understand the definition and characteristics of biblical counseling, we can identify some key mechanics by which biblical counseling operates. Once a person has become a Christian, biblical counseling seeks to help that person progress in their sanctification. The practice of discipleship is applied through biblical counseling. Biblical counseling incorporates the phases of change, the stages of spiritual growth, and the key areas of life where changes take place, into a system to help Christians progress into the sanctification of Jesus Christ. The phases of the change are developed through the stages of spiritual growth. These phases of change and stages of spiritual growth are applied to key areas of life where God holds man accountable to obedience and for disobedience. Through biblical counseling one identifies the phase of change a person is in, in relation to the key areas of life where God holds man accountable to obedience and for disobedience. He then determines the stage of spiritual growth a person is in, in correspondence to the phase of change a person is in. From there, biblical counseling guides the person through that stage of spiritual growth into the next stage of spiritual growth accordingly. This work of biblical counseling is done on a one on one interpersonal level or on a small group level. Let us now explore this further.

Review of The Phases of Change, The Stages of Spiritual Growth, and The Areas of Change

We discovered earlier that there are phases of change by which one grows in the faith. The phases are the normal progression of Christians as they develop through the sanctification process into the likeness of Jesus Christ as empowered by God. For instance, as a Christian is walking by the power of God through the sanctification process there will be a *realization* of Truth as he is being taught by the Word of God. This realization of Truth will lead to a realization of his sin as he is convicted by the

Word of God. The realization of sin will lead to *remorse* over his sin as he is convicted by the Word of God. The remorse over his sin will lead to a *renouncing* of his sin as he follows the Word of God in how to correct his situation. The renouncing of his sin we lead to a *repenting* of his sin as he follows the Word of God in how to correct his situation. The repenting of his sin will lead to *renewing* the mind as he follows the Word of God in how to train in righteousness in his situation. The renewing of the mind will lead to the *replacing* the sin with right living as he follows the Word of God in how to train in righteousness in his situation. This progression is guided by the Holy Spirit who illumines our minds to understand the Scriptures, convicts us of the sin and empowers us to obey accordingly. This is the picture of working out your salvation in fear and trembling as the power of God is working from within (Philippians 2:12-13).

We also discovered that the phases of change are worked out through the stages of spiritual growth. The *teaching stage* of spiritual growth is the stage where one comes to know and understand the truth of God's Word in relation to God, self, others, or situation in order to grow into spiritual maturity in Christ resulting in the realization phase of change. The *conviction stage* of spiritual growth is the stage where one comes to a place of regret leading to remorse through the Word of God as God wills resulting in the remorse phase of change. The *correction stage* of spiritual growth is the stage in which one is learning and progressing in turning from what is wrong in dealing with God, self others, or circumstances resulting in the renouncing phase of change and the repenting phase of change. The *training stage* of spiritual growth is the stage in which one is learning and progressing in walking in what is right to maturity with God, self others, or circumstances as directed by the Word of God resulting in the renewing phase of change and replacing phase of change.

Each phase of change falls under a stage of spiritual growth. Therefore, once we understand the phase of change one is in, we can also understand the stage of spiritual growth one is in. This also helps us to understand the next stage of spiritual growth we need to guide the individual to and through in the discipleship and biblical counseling process. The phrase "stage of spiritual growth" is used to categorize the various phases of change into defined periods of time and is used to determine what has to be done through the Word of God to move someone to or through those particular periods of time. The phrase "phases of change" is a way to explain the steps an individual goes through in the process of change from spiritual birth to spiritual maturity. Knowing this helps us to accomplish our goal of transformation into the likeness of Christ.

In addition, we discovered that in the areas of life where God holds man accountable to obedience and for disobedience are the areas where the phases of change and stages of spiritual growth are applied. God requires man to put off sin and walk in what is right by His power in these areas. When one has a moral, spiritual, immaterial heart, or what the world calls "psychological" or "mental disorders," you will find that the source of the problems and the solution to the problems are traced back to the areas of life where God holds man accountable to obedience and for disobedience. Man is held accountable to obedience and for disobedience in the areas of thoughts, attitudes, intentions, desires, conversation, relationships, and serving of God and others. Every sin problem will be traced back to these areas. All spiritual growth will be traced back to these areas. Consider the problems you have encountered within the last day or so with yourself, with others, or in circumstances. There was not one single problem you encountered that did not include one of those areas where you are held accountable to obedience and for disobedience. Consider the spiritual growth you have seen in your life or the lives of others. Where have you grown spiritually that did not include one of those areas where you are held accountable to obedience and for disobedience? As we understand these areas of accountability we can be effective and efficient in our practice of biblical counseling.

Biblical Counseling and Homework Assignments

In order to guide one through and to stages of spiritual growth within the areas of life where God holds man accountable to obedience and for disobedience, biblical counseling uses homework assignments. Homework assignments are various reading assignments, activities, and projects that are assigned to individuals to help move them through the stages of spiritual growth accordingly, resulting in the various phases of change taking place accordingly in the areas of life where man is held accountable to obedience and for disobedience. Homework assignments can be organized under six basic categories. The six basic categories of homework assignments are hope homework, theological homework, awareness homework, embracing God homework, action oriented homework, and relation oriented homework. These homework assignments are given according to the need of the moment. The phase of change a person is in and the stage of spiritual growth a person is needing to progress to in the areas of life where God hold man accountable to obedience and for disobedience determines the category of homework one is given. These homework assignments aren't random assignments of reading or activities. Neither are these assignments busy work. These assignments are adjusted to fit phases of change and the stage of spiritual growth one needs to go to and through. Homework assignments help individuals to become doers of the Word and not just hearers only. Let us examine each category of homework assignments.

Hope homework assignments are reading assignments, projects, or various activities that seek to help an individual gain hope in the Character and promises of God. Generally this category of homework is applied when individuals are doubting the care of God for them in their situation. It could be as simple as providing someone Scriptures to focus on the various promises of God for their present situation. Another example of hope homework would be to provide individuals with Christian literature to read that teaches on various Characteristics of God and how those characteristics assure that God will always be about our greatest good and His ultimate glory. Or one could be asked to make a list of all the various ways God has protected or provided in the past and present, and then see how that ties to His character that is same yesterday, today, and forevermore. In addition, one could ask the counselee to make a list of all the disappointments they have with God and compare that to the verse that says the hope of the Lord does not disappoint (Romans 5:5) to discover that what they were expecting and what God has promised are completely different. There are many different ways one can apply this category of homework to the lives of people. This category of homework is not connected to any one stage of spiritual growth or phase of change. This category of homework can be applied at all levels. For the unbeliever it can be the avenue by which one comes to hear and embrace the Gospel message of Jesus Christ. For the believer it can be the avenue by which one is reminded of God's care, concern, and love for him.

Theological homework assignments are reading assignments, projects, or various activities that seek to help individuals gain a solid theological understanding of their problems so they can deal with them properly. Sometimes individuals do not understand the biblical reality about their situation. They have been deceived by various psychologies from the ungodly to the point that they do not have a biblical perspective of the situation or problem. In situations like these, one could be provided with a systematic Bible study to read that explains their problem from a biblical perspective. One could be provided with articles or various sections of theology books to read that explain their problem from a biblical perspective. Various literature or audio sermons that define and explain the problem could be suggested for study. Or they could even be asked to interview various individuals in the congregation who have gone through the problem and have come to understand the biblical view of the situation and then write down their findings to be discussed with counselor at a later date. This category of homework is intended to help the individual realize the truth. If one does not realize the truth, he cannot make the necessary changes in his life to please God. He cannot progress through the phases of change and the stages of spiritual growth without realizing the truth. This category of homework is foundational in helping people grow and change.

Awareness homework assignments are reading assignments, projects, or various activities that seek to help individuals gain awareness about their sinfulness so that they would stop deceiving themselves about the problem and begin to deal with it accordingly. Many people are in denial about their sinfulness. Their ritual of righteousness blinds them to the reality of their sinfulness. They may hear truth but yet have no awareness that it is in connection to their own sinfulness. David heard the story from Nathan about the rich man and the poor man but did not connect it to himself (2 Samuel 12: 1-7). Awareness homework bridges the gap between knowing the truth and understanding how it applies to a person in relation to sin and need for change. For example, awareness homework could be an assignment where one has to make a list for a week of every sinful reaction he has in relation to his wife when she does not support him or says something disappointing to him and be ready to discuss the next week.

Another example may be giving someone a list of questions that would help them to evaluate a past experience by answering questions in relation to their thoughts, words, actions, desires, or reactions in connection to the past experience to help stir awareness. Moreover, a person could be sent home with a parable to study and then asked to identify their concerns in relation to the parable while the counselor uses the parable to draw out correlations to the sins of the individual. One cannot change what he does not believe is his problem. Awareness homework is essential for change.

Embracing God homework assignments are reading assignments, projects, or various activities that are used to help people to connect with God according to a particular characteristic of God that relates to their problem or sin. The Bible tells us that without faith it is impossible to please God (Hebrews 11:6). The Bible also tells us anything done without faith is sin (Romans 14:21-23). Every sin problem is a theological problem. Therefore, any sin we commit shows a lack of faith in who God is. We are not talking about a lack of intellectual understanding but a lack of embracing in action what one knows by intellect. Embracing God homework assignments seek to help a person practically embrace a Character or attribute of God to help overcome a sin issue in life. For instance, a person who struggles with anger, worry, or doubt would be connected with reading assignments, memorization assignments, or responsibility assignments that would lead the person to embrace the supremacy, sufficiency, sovereignty, wisdom, and love of God in a real and practical way. A person struggling with pornography or any lust issue may be given practical assignments to help him embrace the holiness and sufficiency of God. If an individual truly accepts in mind and practice that God is first, God is enough for them; God is in control; God knows the best course of action; God is set apart from all that is evil, and God has his best interest at heart, how much anger, worry, doubt, pornography or lust do you think they would walk in consistently? These types of assignments seek to lead the person to walk in genuine fellowship with God.

Action oriented homework assignments are activities and projects given to help individuals put off sinful thoughts, attitudes, intentions, desires, communication patterns, behavioral patterns, relational patterns and serving patterns and to help put on godly thoughts, attitudes, intentions, desires, communication patterns, behavioral patterns, relational patterns and serving patterns. These assignments focus on action. There is no memorization of Scripture or reading. This is the application of Scripture, and reading assignments given. A person may be asked to take a different route home from work to avoid the pornography store that he is tempted by. Or a person may be asked to submit to governing authorities without delay, debate, or discussion on his job for the next five days and write down the experience for discussion with the counselor. In addition, a person may be asked to stop talking about themselves so much in conversation and listen to learn about others through the conversation and write down what they learned about the person for discussion with the counselor. Another example would be asking the individual to serve a complete stranger by meeting some legitimate biblical need without looking for anything in return and write down the experience for discussion with the counselor. This promotes being a doer of the Word of God and keeps counseling from being talk therapy, resulting in leading individuals into the practice of progressive sanctification.

Relationship oriented homework assignments are activities and projects given to help individuals put off unloving relational patterns and put on open and loving relational patterns. These assignments are an extension of the action oriented homework assignments that focus on the central relationships in a person's life. The goal is to help an individual function as God intended within the relationships he has. For example a husband may be given the assignment of making a list of ten observations about his wife and then use those observations as tool of understanding and serving his wife in ten different ways according to that list. Or, a wife may be given the assignment of accepting and following the direction from her husband without debate in five key areas that week. Another example may be for a single person to indentify ten ways to start treating his girlfriend as a sister instead of a lover or wife and begin to practice that for the next ten days. In addition, children may be asked to take the initiative and do things they already know their parents want them to do in advance so that parents do not have to keep telling them to do it over and over again. This moves individuals from talking about the Truth to living the Truth. This is the kind of work that transforms lives and puts the Word of God into the context of real life. This kind of work is crucial for the sanctification process.

Each category of homework assignments is designed to help people through a particular stage of spiritual growth resulting in certain phases of change happening within that stage of spiritual growth. For instance, hope and doctrinal homework assignments are designed to lead individuals to and through the teaching stage of spiritual growth resulting in realization of truth and sin condition according to Scripture. Awareness Homework assignments are designed to lead individuals to and through the conviction stage of spiritual growth resulting in the remorse over sin according to Scripture. Embracing God, action oriented, and relation oriented homework assignments are designed lead individuals to and through the correction stage and training stage of spiritual growth resulting in renouncing of sin, repenting of sin, renewal of mind in the right action to apply and the replacement of sin with right actions according to Scripture.

As the counselor comes to understand the spiritual condition of an individual, he can identify that condition by the stage of spiritual growth the individual is in and by the phases of change the individual needs to walk in. This in turn helps the counselor determine the direction he needs to take in the counseling session as well as the kind of homework he needs to give to facilitate the kind of change that is needed for progressive sanctification. For example, if the counselor identifies that an individual knows and understands that speaking unwholesome words is not good, but does not see that he is the one speaking the unwholesome words, the counselor identifies that this individual is in the teaching stage of spiritual growth because this individual realizes the truth. The counselor's goal would be to lead the individual through the teaching stage of spiritual growth into the conviction of stage of spiritual growth whereby he begins to realize he is the one speaking unwholesome words and would remorse over the sin of it. In order to do this the counselor would prescribe various awareness homework assignments to facilitate the process. This process helps individuals to further in their development of progressive sanctification.

Methods and Homework Assignments

All categories of homework are carried out through various methods which help individuals to develop in their walk with God. Randy Patten who is the Executive Director of NANC (National Association of Nouthetic Counselors) taught me these various methods. We can identify as least six basic methods biblical counselors tend to use:

- Scripture reading– leading individuals into seeing and discovering the reality of God's Word in accordance to their problem; this is done so that individuals may develop a consistent pattern of reading and studying God's Word; this is done so that individuals may understand the nature of God's Word, and live by the content in it in order that they may know God intimately and to be useful to Him practically.

- Literature reading–leading individuals into reading various biblical literature that shows them how to evaluate and address the problem from God's standpoint in a comprehensive manner so that they may turn from sin it and walk in obedience to God accordingly.

- Scripture Memorization–leading individuals into memorizing Scripture so that they may be transformed in their thinking and turn away from sin unto living as God has commanded.

- Prayer–leading individuals into the process of prayer so they may learn how to communicate with God in a way that will lead them into genuine fellowship with God so they my learn how to make request for others and themselves in an appropriate manner.

- Put off/Put On Projects–activities that lead the counselee into stopping some thought, word or action or leading them into starting some thought, word, or action in relation to God, others, self or circumstances as it relates to the issues brought up in the counseling sessions.

- The Log List/Journal method– having the counselee to write down specific thoughts, desires, behaviors, actions or words to evaluate where change has taken place or to see where change needs to take place.

There are many other methods used to facilitate the categories of homework. The goal of any proper method is to lead individuals through realization, remorse, renouncing, repenting, renewing, replacing of sin with right living for God. This is the work of discipleship, starting with the problem.

Concepts to Teach in Biblical Counseling Sessions

As we progress in the work of biblical counseling, we find several basic concepts to be taught throughout the sessions that are essential to helping individuals advance through the stages of spiritual growth and the phases of change in the areas of life where they are held accountable to obedience and for disobedience. The most foundational concept that must be taught is the Gospel. We must present the reality of the person and work of Jesus Christ so that all would clearly receive the message. This is a concept that should not be taken for granted.

We must also teach the basic concept of what people can and cannot control. This will help individuals learn to take responsibility for the areas of life God holds them accountable to obedience and for disobedience. This will help individuals interpret life in manner whereby they no longer blame others for the condition of their own hearts. Another concept that must be taught is the concept of Two Choices in life. My friend Mark Dutton would put this way: "There are only two choices on the shelf: pleasing God or pleasing self." People must understand that the two choices in life are either to be loving or unloving towards God as well as understand the biblical definition of love.

Let's examine a few more concepts that are essential for the advancement of progressive sanctification. We must teach the concept of the biblical framework which is the inner workings of a person's immaterial heart as a result of be loving or unloving towards God and others. When we make the choice of sin, God has put indicators in our immaterial hearts through the conscience such as the awareness of wrong, the fear of judgment, and the desire to flee from the guilty conscience when no one is pursuing or chasing to help us understand that sin has not been confessed, repented of, and replaced in our lives (Genesis 3:1-14, Proverbs 28:1). When we make the choice to love God and love others, God uses the conscience and the Holy Spirit to produce indicators such as the peace of God, confidence before God, and a desire to draw near to God to let us know we are walking rightly before God (Proverbs 28:1, 1John 3:21). Another concept that must be taught is the concept of the four kinds of human relationships found in Proverbs 27:5-6. Sometimes we can be open and unloving—having the right facts but rude in the presentation of facts. Moreover, we can be closed and loving—having a loving heart towards someone but due time constraints, or lack of training one is not able to communicate it. In addition we can be open and loving—right facts and kind presentation of the facts. On the other hand, we can be closed and unloving—pretending to be okay with someone when you are really not okay. This helps individuals evaluate how they are relating to others and make the necessary adjustments.

Let's continue to look at some more key concepts that are helpful for the advancement of progressive sanctification. We should help individuals understand the danger of fearing man as God. Sometimes we place man in the position as the source and solution to life's problems and satisfaction. When that happens we find ourselves making them an idol of worship to obtain the things in this world we crave and love more than God and others. We serve man as we should God in those cases.

Another key concept to teach is the concept of sinful anger. We must help individuals see that anger is an attitude of the mind that moves into emotion and then action. Therefore, it must be dealt with at the heart level first. Anger also exposes that there is something we treasure and the level of lust (James 4:1-3). A few other concepts to consider would be conflict resolution, a biblical view of self esteem, self image, and self-love as well as learning to live a Christ-centered life. These particular concepts are foundational to promoting a lifestyle that glorifies God. They are truly essential for progressive sanctification.

Biblical Counseling and True Hope

Biblical counseling is the only form of counseling that can instill true hope that does not disappoint because it is the hope that comes from God. There are several things to consider. First, biblical counseling promotes hope in the promises of God for our everyday life matters. This is crucial to the individual that doubts that God loves them. It is hard to serve God if you question His care for you. Second, biblical counseling promotes hope in the return of Jesus Christ and the blessings He will bring. This helps us focus on faith in future grace, and helps us to put in perspective the futility of the present pleasures of sin. Third, biblical counseling promotes hope in the rewards of heaven. We can look for and anticipate that our sacrifices for God were not in vain. When Christ returns we know that we will be like Him and that all this pain will one day disappear. This is the real of hope of life because everything else is fading away. True Biblical counseling helps us to set our mind and affections on things to come with Jesus Christ, while we enjoy the blessing below and endure the trials below in a manner worthy of our Lord and Savior Jesus Christ.

The Areas of Change	The Phases of Change	The Stages of Spiritual Growth	Concepts to Teach in the Biblical counseling Sessions	The Homework to help implement Change	The Methods to help implement the homework	The Examples of Implementation of activities
Thoughts (Idea)	Realize truth	*Teaching Stage-* *Realize* truth	The Gospel/ What I Can and Cannot Control	Hope Homework	Scripture Reading	Reading particular Books of the Bible that connect to your issues
Attitude (Belief System that results from a pattern of Ideas)	Realize and Remorse over our Sin in connection with truth	*Conviction Stage-* *Realize* and *Remorse* over our sin in connection with truth	The Two Choices Concept/Inner Workings of Man's Heart as result of making the Two Choices	Theological Homework	Literature Reading	Reading literature that addresses your issues
Intentions	Renounce our Sin	*Correction Stage-* *Renounce* our Sin; *Repent* of our Sin	The Four Kinds of Human Relationships/ The Fear of Man	Awareness Homework	Scripture Memorization	Memorizing and Meditating on Scripture/ Biblical Concepts according to your issues
Communic-ation Patterns	Repent of our Sin	*Training Stage-* *Renew* our minds; *Replace* our Sin with the right thing to do in the areas change	Anger/Conflict Resolution	Embracing God Homework	Prayer	Writing out Log list, or journals to evaluate yourself or your progress
Behavioral and Relational Patterns	Renew our Minds		Biblical View of Self Esteem, Self Image and Self Love	Action Oriented Homework	Projects	Communicating certain things to God or people on a regular basis
Service for God and Others	Replace our Sin with the right thing to do in the areas of change		How to Live a Christ-Centered Life	Relation Oriented Homework	Log List/ Journals/ Church Participation	Practicing certain attitudes, actions or behaviors towards God, others , and in situations/ Getting involved in particular aspects of Church life to enhance growth in Christ

CHAPTER 7

THE 8 "C" s OF BIBLICAL COUNSELING

We have come to understand that the work of biblical counseling is done on a one on one interpersonal level or on a small group level. It is sometimes done on an informal or formal basis. Informal biblical counseling is done in the form of friend to friend talking about matters over dinner, or maybe a coach on a football team giving insight to a player about how to handle a matter with his parents. Formal counseling is done by way of appointments being set up to meet someone in an office to discuss particular matters on a structured session by session process. This is done with pastors or counselors who have set up offices in the church or counseling centers for the purpose of helping people professionally through the Word of God. Whether formal or informal all counseling needs a structure by which to provide the support individuals need. I have had the privilege of being trained by some of the best biblical counselors in the world. Gentlemen such as Dr. Wayne Mack, Dr. Stuart Scott, Dr. John Street, Mr. Randy Patten, and Pastor Rich Thomson. The insights and structure I learned from these men have been foundational to what I teach others. As a result of their teaching, I developed a structure for counseling called the 8 "C" s of counseling which I would like to share with you.

The 8 "C"s of Biblical Counseling

When involved in a biblical counseling session, the counselor can begin the session with the practice of *connecting* with an individual. Connecting involves getting to know the individual before one starts addressing the problems with the individual. The counselor can start connecting by asking the counselee questions that will help him to get to know the counselee better. For instance, you may ask "What has been the most exciting thing that has happen to you this week?" Or you may ask "What has been the most disappointing thing that has happen to you this week? Another way to connect is to seek to find things that you the counselor and the counselee may have in common to discuss to help them to be comfortable. For instance, I may talk about my children with individuals who have children that are my children's age to help them get comfortable talking to me. There are times where I may even discuss hobbies that the counselee and I have in common. Finally, you may want to share areas where you have struggled with the same issue the counselee is seeking to find solutions. This tends to help the counselee find comfort knowing that someone can identify with his issue and can bring real solutions to the matter.

The next step in the session is to begin the process of *consoling* an individual. The counselor consoles the counselee by giving words of encouragement and hope. During this time of the session I teach them 1 Corinthians 10:13. Many have found encouragement through understanding this passage. You can also console the counselee by giving comfort as they share their problems. Sometimes people are comforted by the fact that someone has heard their deep dark secret and did not condemn or condone their issue but gave care accordingly. Consoling is something that will be done through the session. I try to provide it before they begin to share their problems, during the time they are sharing their problems, and after they share their problems. Everyone can benefit from words of encouragement and hope.

After consoling, the counselor may begin the process of *collecting* data from the individual. There are many things the counselor should seek to discover. You want to identify what has happened or is happening to the person. This information helps the counselor identify the areas in life that are beyond the control of the counselee. You want to identify how the counselee has or is responding to what has happened or is happening. This information helps the counselor identify the areas in life that are within the realm of responsibility for the counselee. You want to identify root issues that are the source of the problems. This helps the counselor to distinguish between the issues of the heart and behaviors or actions that stem from the issues of the heart. You want to find the motivations of the heart that are driving the choices of their lives.

As the counselor is collecting data he needs to *categorize* the data into biblical terms and perspectives as he is thinking through biblical solutions. For instance, some talk about codependency but the biblical term is the fear of man. To categorize something according to what it is, helps identify the biblical solution that is the most appropriate for the counselee. You want to distinguish between root sins and fruit sins. For instance, root sins are tied to thoughts, attitudes, motivations, and desires where the sin is conceived. Fruit sins are tied to the sinful behaviors, conversations, relational patterns, and lifestyles that result from the sinful thoughts, attitudes, motivations, and desires. This helps counselor to distinguish between the source of the problem and the symptoms of the problem. Categorization does not solve the problem. But, it does help you organize your thoughts in terms of understanding the problem through biblical lenses.

Once the counselor has collected enough data and categorized it accordingly, the counselor may then begin *communicating* to the counselee what the Bible defines as the source and symptoms of their problems and *clarify* the biblical solutions to those problems. This is where the counselor teaches the counselee from Scripture. You help him/her gain a biblical insight on the issues. As the counselor, you are seeking to deal with people according to their position and condition. As the counselor, you are focusing on salvation and sanctification. You focus on salvation if they are in position of sinner which means their condition is one of spiritual death in need of spiritual life (the Gospel). As the counselor, you focus is sanctification if they are in position of Saint which means their condition is one of spiritual life in need of development (Discipleship). Your understanding of the phases of change and the stages of spiritual growth will be helpful in this step of the counseling session. That understanding will help the counselor to think through what to say and how to say it to the individual in counseling at that time.

After the counselor has communicated the problems and clarified the solutions, he may begin *challenging* the individual to make changes accordingly. This step is assumed more than applied. We tend to believe that when people come to counseling they want to change. Generally, people aren't looking to change; they are looking to change someone else or something else. In other words, they are not looking to repent and replace. People tend to look for relief. When challenging the counselee you want to help them understand that in order for them to be and to function as God intended requires their commitment to train and disciplines themselves in the application of the Word of God in accordance to the issues at hand. This is where the "fork in road" begins. The counselee has to decide if they are going to work hard or do nothing. You the counselor will be able to determine at this point if counseling will continue or not. If they are unwilling to do the work, counseling cannot continue, but if they are willing to do the work, counseling can continue.

After the counselor has challenged the individual to make changes accordingly he has to *construct* homework assignments to help the counselee change accordingly if they accept the challenge. This is where the counselor's understanding of the categories of homework will be helpful (See Chapter 6). For instance if you know your counselee is in the teaching stage of spiritual growth in relation to the problem you may give them doctrinal homework and awareness homework to move them into the conviction stage of spiritual growth. Or, if you the counselor know your counselee is in the conviction stage of spiritual growth you may give them embracing God, action oriented, or relational oriented homework in order to move them into correction and training stages of spiritual growth in those areas discussed in counseling. Homework needs to be specific and practical.

In other words, the assignments must connect to the problem in such a manner that the individual is able to put off the sin and put on the right way of living accordingly. The counselor must assign homework that fits not only the context of the problem but also the context of the individual's life. You must take into account the counselee's work schedule, home life, and other responsibilities when assigning homework. There must also be a challenge to those individuals about changing some of those things to work on the homework.

After the counselor has constructed homework for individuals who accept the challenge for change, he may begin *conjoining* the counselee to the local church accordingly. Individuals must be connected to the body according the five "m"s. The counselee must be connected to membership, maturity, magnification, ministry, and missions according to their specific need. Since the church is the counseling ministry, individuals need to be connected to that community in order to get the full effect of the counseling ministry. Remember as Steve Viars has put it "You can't have an effective counseling ministry until you have a ministry that counsels." The counselee's change happens in the community not necessarily in the counseling session. There may be times where an individual may be so involved that they have become distracted from the purpose of involvement in the Body of Christ. This may require the counselee to step back from involvement in order to evaluate what is happening in their lives. For instance, one may be too heavily involved in the ministry aspect of the church that they are not spending enough time in the maturity and membership aspect of the church. You must guide the counselee through this process accordingly.

The Kinds of People Counselors Come in Contact with in Counseling

When counseling individuals, sometimes counselors will come in contact with individuals who just need biblical knowledge on the matter and can figure out how to apply the biblical knowledge to the matter on their own. This group of people is a jewel to work with. They tend to be trained in applying the Word of God to their lives. This group of people does not require a lot time just quick information. Second, counselors may come in contact with individuals who have biblical knowledge on a matter but refuse to apply that knowledge to address the matter. This is not immaturity; this is stubbornness! This group of people refuses to do what they know. They require loving correction and rebuke for their unwillingness to do what is right.

In addition to the kinds of people mentioned above, There are two other categories of people counselors tend to come into contact with in counseling. Sometimes counselors come in contact with individuals who have bible knowledge on a matter, but do not know how to apply that knowledge to their situation. This set of people does not need more information from you. They need application assignments. These individuals need "how to" wisdom as a opposed to "what to" information. As the counselor, you need to be skilled in practical application when dealing with this kind of people. Finally, counselors tend to come in contact with individuals who have no bible knowledge on a matter and do not care to learn what to apply or how to apply biblical knowledge to the matter. People like this are more than likely unbelievers who need the Gospel.

What to Look for in a Counseling Session

Throughout the counseling session the counselor needs look for the central issues that need to be addressed in relation to the areas where God holds man accountable to obedience and for disobedience. For instance, you would seek evaluate thoughts, attitudes, motives, or desires. The counselor would also seek to evaluate communication patterns, behavioral patterns, relational patterns or serving patterns. Throughout the counseling session the counselor is seeking to determine what stage of spiritual growth the counselee is in and what stage he needs to go to in relation to the areas where God holds man accountable to obedience and for disobedience. For instance, if the person is in the teaching stage in their communication patterns the counselor would seek to move them through the teaching stage into the conviction stage. Finally, throughout the counseling session, the counselor would seek to evaluate what the counselee can and cannot control. As a counselee learns to distinguish between them, they will find success in living a life of accepting what God allows while living according to what God says.

Knowing Your Position, Heart and Responsibility in a Counseling Session

The counselor is not the change agent but an instrument in the hand of God that facilitates change. If the counselor lacks patience or gets irritated with people in counseling then he has made counseling a personal issue. When that happens, the counselor may be consumed with the outcome of someone's change as being a reflection of their abilities or lack thereof to effectively counsel. It could also be that someone's change or lack thereof results in a benefit or detriment to the counselor accordingly. Or it could mean that counselee has the same weakness as the counselor. As a result the counselor has been ignoring it in himself while being hyper-critical of it in others. The counselor must accept responsibility for personal sin matters that may arise while counseling others. The counselor must consider it is as an opportunity for personal development in spiritual maturity as they learn to serve someone else in the same process.

Eight "C"s of Biblical Counseling

1. **_Connect_** with the counselee in the first part of the counseling session.
   a. Ask your counselee questions that will help you to get to know them better.
   b. Identify areas of common interest and share those with the counselee.
   c. Share things about yourself that you think will lead your counselee to be comfortable with you (Proverbs 16:24)).

2. **_Console_** the Counselee during the counseling session.
   a. Give words of hope and encouragement to assure the counselee that God has solutions to his problem.
   b. Provide comfort as the counselee shares their problems and concerns.
   c. Be compassionate and patient as your counselee shares his heart with you.

3. **_Collect_** data from the Counselee in regards to his problems and concerns.
   a. Find out what is happening or has happened to the person.

b. Find out how he is responding in thought, words, behavior, lifestyle, relational patterns to what is happening or has happened.

c. Identify time frame of responses to people, places, events in accordance to what is happening or has happened.

d. Find out what they want that they cannot control getting and what they are getting they do not want.

e. Identify areas of anger, worry, or fear.

f. Find out what the person's perceptions, preferences, pains, passions are in connection to what is happening or has happened.

d. Find out how he has dealt with or is dealing with sin towards God and others.

e. Look for any and all unloving thoughts, words, and actions.

4. ***Categorize*** data from the Counselee into Biblical terms and perspectives as you are thinking through Biblical solutions.

a. Where there is a biblical term or interpretation for the data use it in place of psychological terms so that those issues may be dealt with accordingly.

b. Identify and interpret thoughts, words, feelings or actions that express a form of fleeing when no one is chasing as such when you are collecting the data (Proverbs 28:1).

c. Identify and interpret thoughts, words, feelings or actions that express a form of fear of God's judgment as such when you are collecting the data (Genesis 3:8-10).

d. Identify and interpret thoughts, words, feelings or actions that express or demonstrate a guilty conscience as such when you are collecting the data (1John 3:21).

e. Identify and interpret root sins and sins that come out of those sins (fruit sins) as such when you are collecting the data.

f. Identify and interpret what a person can and cannot control in their situation past, present, future as you are collecting the data.

g. Identify and interpret their conduct, character, and conversation according to Biblical perspectives.

5. **Communicate** to Counselee what the Bible defines as the source and the symptoms of the problems in Biblical terms and clarify what the Biblical solutions are to those Problems. Here are some examples to consider:

a. Explain the concept of a lack of love for God and others and the solution of love.

b. Explain the concept of root and fruit sins and the solution to this.

c. Explain the concept of worshipping the creation above the creator and the solution.

d. Explain the concept of progressive sanctification.

e. Explain the concept of confession, repentance, and replacement of sin.

f. Explain the concept of how man sins from the immaterial heart which works itself out in the use of the body to carry out those actions.

g. Explain the concept of guilt and the standards of the conscience.

h. Explain the four kinds of human relationships.

i. Explain the fear of man, anger, worry, anxiety and the solutions.

j. Explain the concept of pride and the solutions.

k. Explain the concept of embracing God according to who He is to overcome sin in life.

l. Explain the concept of what a man can and cannot control and how to work through that in a practical manner.

m. Explain the concept of being controlled by the Holy Spirit.

6. *__Challenge__* the Counselee to a commitment to confess, repent, and replace sin with love for God and others.

a. Ask the counselee if they are willing to do the hard work of confessing, repenting, and replacing sin to walk in love for God and others.

b. Explain to the counselee the importance of being a doer of the Word and not just a hearer of the Word.

c. Explain what kind of commitment it will take to make the appropriate changes to resolve the problem and become Godly in the situation.

7. __Construct__ homework for the counselee to apply to their lives that will lead them into confession, repentance, and replacement of sin with love for God and others

a. *__Hope Homework__* – projects, activities and reading assignments given to help people gain a true hope in Christ in accordance to the problems they are facing.

b. *__Doctrinal Homework__* – projects, activities, and reading assignments given to help people gain a solid theological understanding of their problems so that they can deal with them properly.

c. *__Awareness Homework__* – projects, activities, and reading assignments given to help people become aware of their own sinfulness in the problem so that they can stop deceiving themselves about the problem they are facing and own up to it accordingly.

d. *__Embracing God Homework__* – projects, activities, and reading assignments given to help people to connect with God according to a particular characteristic of God that relates to their problem or sin.

e. *__Action Oriented Homework__* – projects and activities that lead people to put off particular sinful thoughts, desires, conversations, behavior, and lifestyle and to put on particular godly thoughts, desires, conversations, behavior, and lifestyle according to the situation or problem.

f. ***Relational Orientated Homework*** – projects and activities that lead people to put off unloving relational patterns and move them to relate in open and loving relational patterns towards others within the situation or problem and abroad.

g. (Portions of this information was adapted from <u>Instruments in a Redeemer's Hand</u> by Paul Tripp).

8. ***Conjoin*** the counselee to the Body of Christ according to where they need it.
   1. *Membership* – the counselee would be lead to join a local church that they may experience love and enjoy the blessings of God-honoring relationships .
   2. *Maturity* – the counselee would be lead to get involved in discipleship courses in a local Church that would lead them into loving God, loving others on a consistent basis and living a life that reflects the character of Christ.
   3. *Magnification* – the counselee would be led to come to appreciate, value and adore the character of God through heart-felt genuine worship of Him in a local Church.
   4. *Ministry* – the counselee would be led to join a ministry where they can develop in bearing burdens and meeting needs according to the various relationships they will develop through the local Church.
   f. *Missions* – the counselee would be led into supporting a local Church in sharing and defending the Christian faith.

Every Christian a Counselor
Chapter 8
Developing a Infrastructure for Biblical Counseling

We have defined biblical counseling and have evaluated some key mechanics of biblical counseling. We have identified a structure by which you can practice biblical counseling whether it is formal or informal. We now want to provide a way by which you can structure a biblical counseling ministry within the local setting of your church. There are a few components that are fundamental to setting up a viable counseling ministry. These are components that help to define the ministry and explain how the ministry should operate. Remember this is a way, not the way. You may look at this and consider another way to do things. That is great. The intent is to give you a tool that you can use accordingly within the context of your local church. Consider developing a purpose statement, objectives, structure, ministry descriptions, and process within the structure to define the ministry and explain the process of how the biblical counseling ministry should operate within the context of your local congregation along with how it will train and reproduce workers for the ministry.

Purpose and Objectives for a Biblical Counseling Ministry

When developing a biblical counseling ministry you want to have a purpose statement. The purpose statement defines the mission of the ministry. It explains why the ministry exists. An example of a purpose statement would be: "To assist individuals with various problems and concerns through the Word of God as well as train, develop and equip people to serve in this ministry according to the Word of God." From this statement there is no doubt or misunderstanding as to why this ministry exists. The purpose statement keeps the focus of the ministry in mind. Many ministries began to dabble into areas that do not fit their original design because they did not clearly define their mission. If you have developed a counseling ministry without clearly defining its mission this is the time to do so. If you have developed a counseling ministry with a clearly defined mission, review the purpose statement and see does it fit what is currently happening in the ministry. If it does fit, praise God. If it does not, find out what went wrong.

Another key element to developing a counseling ministry is to develop clear objectives for the ministry. Objectives define and explain what you want to accomplish in relation to your purpose. As the purpose statement tells why the ministry exist, the objectives explain what the ministry plans to do on a consistent basis to accomplish your mission. The objectives are the over-arching goals that never change. When these over-arching goals are accomplished, they fulfill the purpose of the ministry. An example of an objective would be "To provide biblical answers and solutions to people dealing with marital problems, mental disorders, crisis issues, general matters, and parenting problems." Another example would be "To train leaders, laymen, and other churches in the discipline of biblical counseling through various workshops, training courses, videos, and guest lecturers. These objectives define the direction the ministry will take to fulfill the purpose for which it exists. These objectives are realistic and attainable. It is futile to develop unrealistic objectives. Without having a purpose and objectives to accomplish the purpose, the ministry has no clear direction.

The Structure and Ministry Descriptions For a Biblical Counseling Ministry

In establishing a counseling ministry, you want to establish a structure by which the ministry will operate. The structure shows how the ministry will be organized to function according to its purpose and objectives and identifies the various areas of focus or departments needed in order for the ministry to function according to its purpose and objectives. For example, the ministry can have an organizational chart which clearly shows the structure of the ministry. There could be the assimilation department that focuses on connecting individuals who come for counseling to the right area and person to counsel them. There could be a department of marriage and family that focuses on dealing with people who are having marriage problems, parenting problems, or who are seeking pre-marital counseling. There could be a department of crisis that focuses on dealing with people who have been raped, abused, molested, considering suicide, or just lost their job, home etc. There could be a department of mental disorders that focuses on providing deep biblical answers and solutions to people dealing with bipolar, conversion disorders, depression, or any of the various mental disorders the world has labeled as such. There could be a department of sexual worship disorders and substance worship disorders to address those who are deep in sexual sin or abusing drugs with clear cut biblical answers and solutions. There could be a department of general issues that deals with basic decision making issues or minor problems in life along with the training department that will focus on training people to serve in biblical counseling. These areas of focus show how the ministry will be organized to accomplish its purpose and objectives.

As the structure is clear, there must be a developing of particular roles and responsibilities to accomplish the purpose and objectives within the structure that has been developed. These are the job descriptions or what we can call "ministry descriptions" that define and explain the various roles and responsibilities of individuals participating within their area of focus within the ministry. For instance, you could have a director of the ministry, assistant director, administrative assistants, team leader of assimilation area, assimilation counselors, team leader of marriage and family area, marriage and family counselors, team leader of crisis area, crisis counselors, team leader of worship disorder areas, sexual and substances worship disorder counselors, team leader of general issues area, general issues counselors, and team leader of biblical counseling training area along with biblical counseling trainers. For each of these particular areas of focus you would need to identify things such as position title, purpose of position, who they report to, what they are responsible for, spiritual gifts, talents, strengths needed to fulfill responsibilities in area of focus, and measurable goals to determine if one is fulfilling his/her responsibilities in area of focus. This leaves no room for ambiguity in relation to one's task. As I worked with Dr. Ivory Varner of Bible Way Fellowship Church in Houston, Texas, he taught me how to structure ministries in this manner. This frame has helped me to structure ministries and restructure ministries accordingly. I am truly grateful for his teaching because I am able to pass this to you. The categories I gave are "a way" not "the way". You may find that within the context of your ministry there is another way to approach it. No matter what you do, make sure your roles and responsibilities are clearly defined.

The Process of Operation for a Biblical Counseling Ministry

The next step after these things are developed is to lay out a process by which all these areas work together to service the church and or the local community. This step helps individuals understand how the ministry functions from a big picture perspective. This step shows the logical sequence of what happens when a person comes to get help. For example: Individuals coming for counseling will call the office or come by the ministry area → then an assimilation counselor will set up a time to meet with them to determine how the ministry can best serve the individuals; → the assimilation counselor will meet with individuals and direct them to the area of counseling that will best serve their needs; → the counselor will serve them according to the area of expertise by using the Word of God without any psychological principles or integration of secular thought in their counseling process. This will help to clarify in simple terms the way the ministry will fulfill its purpose and objectives. For some, knowing the purpose and objectives does not bring clarification as to how the ministry works. However, when you show them the process it helps them understand. The process does not have to be long and detailed; rather it should be short and simple. You do not want people to get bogged down with details. This part of the set up should help individuals see how the ministry operates in a clear and concise manner.

As you put together the operating procedures for the biblical counseling ministry there are a few items you want to make sure that you have in place. You want to make sure that the biblical counseling ministry operates using a personal data inventory. A personal data inventory is a form that allows the person coming for counseling to put pertinent information down on paper. Things such as the number of siblings one has, health issues, church attendance, the reason for coming to counseling, belief about sin, and many others pertinent issues are documented. This helps the counselor gain information before the counseling session so that he can be equipped for the session. As the counselor learns how to use this personal data inventory properly, he/she could save a lot of time in the counseling process. For instance, if someone is able to tell you on the personal data inventory what they believe about sin and how they deal with sin, you can determine by their answer what needs to be done. There are many types of personal data inventories out there you can use, or you can create your own. The important point is that your counseling ministry should not operate without one. Every individual must be instructed in the policy that no counseling will take place until the personal data inventory is completed.

Another item that is key to your counseling ministry is a consent to counsel with release of liability form. This is a legal form that you have a lawyer draw up that explains the terms and conditions of biblical counseling at your congregation. Part of the terms and conditions you would have the lawyer draw up would be a willingness to settle any disputes that may occur outside the court systems and within Christian mediation. Another part of the terms and conditions you would have the lawyer draw up would be an explanation of what state laws the church must comply with in relation to reporting child abuse, criminal issues or matters where one is called to report. Within the terms and conditions would be a place for individuals to sign stating they agree with the terms and conditions and would release liability accordingly. In addition, the document would explain how your counseling is strictly biblical and does not involve psychological principles, concepts, or terms. Moreover, the document would explain how your counseling does not use secular humanistic models that require one to be licensed by the state to practice. You cannot control someone seeking to sue, but you can seek to limit the potential as much as possible by making it clear that no counseling will take place until the form is signed by the individual(s) seeking counseling from the ministry. You would need to discuss these matters in detail with a lawyer so that you would know how specific this document should and should not be. Peacemaker Ministries is a ministry organized by Ken Sande to help in matters such as these. I would suggest you contact this ministry to provide details on how to properly put this part together in a way that fits the context of your ministry.

Another key item that is essential to your counseling ministry is an in-session counseling form. The in-session counseling form is used to document activity that is happening during the counseling session. For example, as the counselor is collecting data and categorizing data this information is placed on the in-session counseling form accordingly. The in-session counseling form could have reminders of information that may need to be presented or even categories of homework that may be need to be given accordingly. No matter how the form is structured, it becomes the standard for documenting and working through a session with individuals. This form is for the counselor's personal use and not necessarily for documentation to be filed. The in-session counseling form would be a support tool for the counselor to help him/her stay on track within the counseling sessions. I have found this tool to be very helpful in the process of counseling. I have seen different in-session counseling forms over the years. They all emphasize whatever the designer thought was important for the counselor to focus on or to remember. As you find or develop an in-session counseling form, you want to make sure that it emphasizes what you want your counselors to focus on within the context of your ministry.

Another key item that is essential for your counseling ministry is a case report form. A case report form documents the whole session in a big picture. The case report form documents things such as time, date, the number of the session, what the person came for, what issues where addressed, the Scriptures that were given, the solutions that were given, the homework assignments given, and the hope that was given in the session, as well as future assignments that will be given. This information would be documented on the case report form for every counseling session that takes place with the individual(s). This information would be put in a private area along with the consent to counsel, release of liability form, and personal data inventory of the individual(s) that came for counseling. Imagine if a counselor within the ministry could no longer serve the individual(s) for whatever reason. The ministry could assign someone else to the case with clear, concise information on where things were left off and where things need to go. The ministry would be able to continue to serve the individual(s) accordingly. The case report form would be a required document that every counselor would need to fill out after every counseling session. This form would be vital to the ministry. The forms would need to be kept in a place where there is limited access and where no one can access without some form of security clearance within the ministry.

The Training of Biblical Counselors in Your Local Assembly

This kind of ministry requires extensive training of individuals in the area of biblical counseling. The church needs to identify a biblical counseling ministry that can be used to help start the initial training or developing of individuals within the ministry. Organizations such National Association of Nouthetic Counseling (NANC), Christian Counseling Education Foundation (CCEF), or Faith Baptist Church in Lafayette, Indiana are foundational organizations that can be contacted to help start and implement your biblical counseling ministry. Before individuals are being trained in the area of biblical counseling there needs to be a plan to identify a director of the ministry, an assistant director of the ministry, administrative assistants, trainers who will create or adapt a counseling training curriculum that will continue to train future counselors within the church, and counselors who will serve accordingly. The biblical counseling training will be futile if there is no team to implement the process. In addition, the biblical counseling training will be futile if the leadership of the church is not sold out and leading the charge of this ministry. Moreover, the biblical counseling training will be futile if the biblical counseling ministry is not seen as a ministry that helps to facilitate the work of evangelism of discipleship on a interpersonal, small group level. Furthermore, the biblical counseling training will be futile if there is no organized discipleship system within the local assembly. All these factors must be considered and in place before one can even consider pursing biblical counseling training. Remember you cannot have an effective counseling ministry until you have church ministry that counsels.

EVERY CHRISTIAN A COUNSELOR
CHAPTER 9
ESSENTIALS FOR BUILDING A GOD-HONORING CHURCH

As we have stated in previous chapters, God is saving souls and maturing saints unto the image of Jesus Christ through the church's work of evangelism and discipleship as each individual of the church functions according to his spiritual gifts within the local assembly. Church development must revolve around these key essential priorities. Out of these priorities should flow some essential elements that will lead the church to be the kind of ministry that functions efficiently and effectively. In this chapter we would like to present to you an example of how you can begin to define and direct your church so that it may be organized and structured in such a manner that you can become a church that counsels, resulting in a efficient and effective counseling ministry.

The Essential Priorities of the Church

1. God is saving souls from hell and maturing saints into the image of Christ (Ephesians 2:1-10, 2 Corinthians 3:17-18).

2. God is using the Church through evangelism and discipleship in order to save souls from hell and mature saints into the image of Christ (Matthew 28:18-20, 2 Corinthians 5:15 20, Ephesians 4:11-17).

3. God is using individuals within the Church through their spiritual gifts which results in burdens being bared, needs being met, and truth being proclaimed which results in evangelism and discipleship taking place resulting in souls being saved from hell and saints being matured into the image of Christ (Romans 12:3-8, 1 Peter 4:10-11, Ephesians 4:15-16).

4. In order for a Church to function as God intended the essentials priorities must be evangelism and discipleship.

The Essential Point of the Church: Developing Christ Centered Lives

Step 1
Salvation
Through a literal crucifxtion on on the Cross, death, burial and resurection from the dead as result of that literial cricifixtion, Jesus Christ paid the penalty of the sin debt that all mankind owes to God.
You will be saved from the penalty of sin the power of sin and one day the presence of sin and saved unto a genuine relationship with God if you repent of sin and put a genuine trust/belief in Jesus Christ as Savior from the penalty of your sin and Lord of your life

Step 2
Sanctification
As result of one's salvation , one should seek to turn from Self reliance, Sin and God replacements to develop in Chrislike Character, Conduct, and Conversation through genunine fellowship and obedience to Jesus Christ as He uses His, power, people and circumstances to tranform you unto His Image

Step 3
Service
There must be a commitment to serve as an Ambassador to Unbelievers (Evangelsim) and to serve as a Builder to Believers (Discipleship) using your Spiritual gifts to bear burdens, meet needs and proclam the truth which will resulit in learning to love people, to know what their issues are, to speak the truth in love as it relates to those issues and to lead them to do some thing about those issues as it relates to either salvation or sanctification

Summation
Through your Salvation, Sanctifiction, and Service, God will use you to bring People :
To Believe in Jesus Christ
To Belong to the Community of Jesus Christ (The Body of Believers)
To Become like Jesus Christ through His Community (The Body of Believers)

The Essential Ingrediants to a Genuine Christ Centered Life

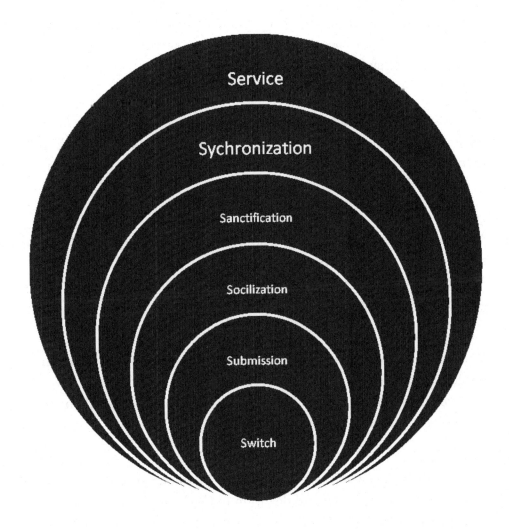

The Essential Ingrediants to a Genuine Christ Centered Life

Switch
- A person must be justified in Jesus Christ–legally declared free from the penalty of sin through faith in person and work of Jesus Christ; moved from the position of sinner to Saint in Jesus Christ (a switch in position).
- A person must be regenerated by Jesus Christ–a heart(mind, will, affections, conscience) that has been transformed from spiritual death to spiritual life in Jesus Christ (a switch in the heart).

Submission
- As a result of the switch, one is to surrender to Jesus Christ as Lord and Savior.
- As a result of the switch, one is to submit to the authority and follow the instructions of Jesus Christ.

Socialization
- As a result of the switch, one is to seek to know Jesus Christ intimately, socializing with Him more than ever before.
- As a result of the switch, one is to seek to be genuinely devoted to Jesus Christ socializing with Him more than ever before.

Sanctification
- As a result of the switch, one is to seek to set himself apart from sin in character, conduct, conversation and commitments.
- As a result of the switch, one is to seek to pursue Christ-likeness in character, conduct, conversation and commitments.

Synchronization
- As a result of the switch, one is to seek to be in one accord with fellow Christians while pursuing single-minded devotion to Christ and His agenda.
- As a result of the switch, one is to seek to maintain love with other Christians while pursuing single-minded devotion to Christ and His agenda.

Service
- As a result of the switch, one is to be an ambassador to unbelievers.
- As a result of the switch, one is to be a builder to believers.

The Essential Practice of the Church

Step 1 Mission—going out into the community, city, state, country, and world to make Disciples of Jesus Christ.

Step 2 Membership—building genuine relationships with one another within the local body and bringing those people we have lead to become disciples through our evangelism into genuine relationship with us and others within the local body of Christ; holding one another accountable to live accordingly in Jesus Christ.

Step 3 Maturity—teaching the members within the local assembly who God is, what He requires, who we are in Christ, how to function according to our new position, power, purity, purpose, and passion in Jesus Christ; how to put off a life of sin and put on life of righteousness according to our faith in Jesus Christ; helping members develop in the application of these things; teaching members the doctrines, disciplines, duties, and demographics of the Christian faith and helping them develop in application of these things accordingly.

Step 4 Magnification—teaching members how to embrace and to genuinely worship God according to who He is in character and what He has done; helping them grow in true worship.

Step 5 Ministry— helping members to discover their spiritual gifts, leading them to use their spiritual gifts to bear burdens and meet needs of one another within the local assembly; helping members to become builders of the body of Christ and ambassadors to the world for Christ.

The Essential Steps to Developing A Church

STEP I – Establish the Essential Priorities, Point and Practice of the Church

The Essential Priorities of the Church: To develop and maintain a church that revolves around the work of Evangelism and Discipleship so that God will use the church to bring about His work of Salvation and Sanctification through it

The Essential Point of the Church: To lead members into complete maturity in Jesus Christ resulting in members being Christ-Centered and living Christ-Centered Lives in all aspects

The Essential Practice of the Church:

Mission- being Ambassadors to unbelievers by sharing the Gospel of Jesus Christ in the community, city, state, country, and the world

Membership- connecting with one another in small groups and in corporate gatherings to build genuine relationships, and to hold one another accountable to love and good deeds

Maturity- teaching and mentoring individuals through the Word of God in small groups, centralized courses, and corporate gatherings so that members would grow to complete maturity in Jesus Christ resulting in members being Christ-Centered and living Christ-Centered lives in all aspects

Magnification-worshiping the Lord in small groups and corporate gathering in spirit and truth according to who He is, what He has done and what He will do

Ministry- being Builders of the Body of Christ by using our spiritual gifts, talents and treasures to bear burdens, meet needs, and provide the truth with the goal of building a spiritually healthy and mature set of believers within the local assembly

STEP II - Organize Leadership Roles and Responsibilities Accordingly

Elders- policy makers, strategic planning, managing the church, mentoring other leaders, church discipline issues

Associate Pastors- pulpit support, preaching funerals, counseling, wedding ceremonies, teaching, leading over various ministries

Deacons- communion, benevolence, funeral coordination, home visitations, hospital visitations, sick and shut in support, transportation coordination and building and grounds upkeep etc.

Director of Ministries- manage, administrate, oversee, direct the six key areas of ministry of the Church as well as the ministries that fall under those six key areas of ministry

Team Leaders/Coordinators- manage, administrate, oversee, direct specific areas in ministries that fall under the six key ministries of the Church

STEP III - Organize Ministry Structure Into Six Key Ministries of the Church

Management- all ministries that focus on administration, finances, maintenance, or marketing will fall under this Ministry

Membership- all ministries pertaining to church fellowship, visitation, and connecting people will fall under this Ministry

Magnification- all ministries that are tied to Sunday morning worship services and Wednesday night worship services as well as prayer ministries will fall under this Ministry.

Maturity- all ministries that focus on helping individuals grow into spiritual maturity will fall under this Ministry

Ministry- all ministries that focus on bearing burdens and meeting needs of the local Church body will fall under this Ministry

Missions- all ministries that focus on reaching out to save the lost and providing benefits to the poor and needy outside the Church will fall under this Ministry.

STEP IV- Develop an Assimilation Process to Move People from Membership to Missions

Membership Seminar- all persons interested in becoming a member of the Church will be directed to the Membership Seminar. If they agree with Church –By laws, vision ,direction and doctrine of the Church they will sign a Membership Covenant and become members if approved by Elders. They will then be placed in a small group according to their demographic.

Maturity Seminar- all who become members must attend the Maturity Seminar whereby they will learn the process of spiritual growth and our process of discipleship. If they agree to our process they sign a Maturity Covenant which affirms their willingness to be a disciple and take courses accordingly

Ministry Seminar- all who become members must attend the Ministry Seminar whereby they will learn the Doctrine of Spiritual Gifts and the importance of serving in a ministry according to their gifts. Afterwards, each person will take a spiritual gift assessment to help them to determine where they are gifted.

Then they will sign a Ministry Covenant which affirms their commitment to use their gifts to serve others in the Body and abroad. Afterwards they will be guided into to selecting a ministry to serve in according to their giftedness, passion, and time constraints.

Missions Seminar- all who become members must attend the Missions Seminar whereby they will learn our strategy and structure for reaching out to save the lost and provide benefits to the poor and needy outside the church. They will then be challenged to join our efforts to reach out. They then will sign a Missions Covenant which affirms their commitment to join us in reaching out to the lost. Afterwards, they will select at least 4 events they will participate in and continue to sign up to at least two a year as part of their commitment to the Church.

STEP V - Develop and Structure Small Groups According to Demographics

Marriage Ministry- a ministry that will bear the burdens, meet the needs, and disciple married couples of all ages in the Church

Men's Ministry- a ministry that will bear the burdens, meet the needs, and disciple men in the Church

Women's Ministry- a ministry that will bear the burdens meet the needs, and disciple women in the Church

Young Adult/Career Ministry- a ministry that will bear the burdens, meet the needs, and disciple Young Adults in college and out of college starting new careers attending the Church

Youth Ministry- a ministry that will bear the burdens, meet the needs, and disciple youth between the ages of 13-18.

Children's Ministry- a ministry that will bear the burdens, meet the needs, and disciple children 12 and under

Golden Age Ministry- a ministry that will bear the burdens, meet the needs and disciple seniors citizens

STEP VI - Develop a Discipleship Training Structure, Process, and Courses

Sunday Morning

a. Doctrines/Disciplines/Duties of the Christian
   Faith Courses

b. Demographic Sunday School Classes(Men, Women,
   Marriage, Young Adult, Teen, Children, Golden Age etc.)

Wednesday Night

a. Doctrines/Disciplines/Duties of the
   Christian Faith Courses

b. Demographic Bible Studies

c. Youth Topic Current Issues/Doctrinal
   Courses

d. Awana Ministry for Children

STEP VII - Develop a Leadership Training Program

Elders- Train future elders through the book and workbook <u>Biblical Eldership</u> by Alexander Strauch, Biblical Counseling Training, along with some practical ministry experience according to the position

Associate Pastors- Train future Pastors who may not be able to take on the Elder Role through the books <u>Shepherding God's Flock</u> by Jay Adams and <u>Rediscovering Pastoral Ministry</u> by John MacArthur Jr., Biblical Counseling Training, along with some practical ministry experience according to the position

Deacons- train future deacons according to the book <u>New Testament Deacon</u> by Alexander Strauch, Biblical Counseling Training, along with practical ministry experience according to the position

Director of Ministries- use various leadership books and biblical characters to train directors in how to manage and lead according to the needs of the ministry; make sure they are trained in Biblical Counseling, provide practical ministry experience according to the position

Team Leaders/Coordinators- use various leadership books and biblical characters to train directors in how manage and lead according to the needs of the ministry; make sure they are trained in Biblical Counseling; provide practical ministry experience according to the position

STEP VIII - Develop a Biblical Counseling Training Center

In-House Training- provide a curriculum and practical training process to teach all leaders and interested members in the process of Biblical Counseling

Overall Training- provide training to individuals outside the church who are interested in how to practice Biblical Counseling

Church Counseling Services- provide counseling services to body as needed

Community Counseling Services- provide counseling services to the community as needed

STEP IX - Develop Strategic Fellowship Times for Church Body

Party with the Pastor- Establish a time on a regular basis during the year whereby the Members get to hang out with the Pastors/Elders for food, fun, fellowship and question and answer

Church Picnic- Establish a time on a regular basis whereby the church gets to together for food, fun, and fellowship

Christmas Program- a time whereby the Church comes together and celebrate the Birth of Christ through some form of play or production

Church Carnival- Establish annual carnival whereby the community can come and enjoy festivities according to specific themes that will be developed annually

Thanksgiving Dinner- a time whereby the Church comes together to give thanks to God for all He has done through praise, testimonies, preaching, fellowshipping and eating

STEP X - Develop Strategic Mission Plan

Short Term Missions- Identify where we will go overseas and who we will send for a short-term missions trip

Long Term Missions- Identify where we will go overseas and who we will send or will support on a long term missions trip

Bridging Events- Identify various events the Church could provide that would develop a bridge to connect the Church to the community that we may share the Gospel and demonstrate the love of Christ

STEP XI - Develop a Strategic Marketing Plan

22 Touch Program- a system that is developed to help us connect with visitors at least 22 times a year through various means such as phone calls, cards, e-mails, visitations etc.

Devotional Books- provide the community with devotional books based on a sermon series to be preached during that time

Gifts- every person who visits more than twice will receive some kind of book, tape or gift certificate as a token of our appreciation for visiting

Advertising- take out ads in various newspapers and newsletters as well as radio and TV spots

Promotion of Bridging Events- makes sure direct mail and all other avenues pursued to promote various events

Signs – purchase signs which tell times and location of Church services

Direct Mail – purchase addresses from various services and do direct mailing to invite people to visit our Church

The Essential Structure of the Church

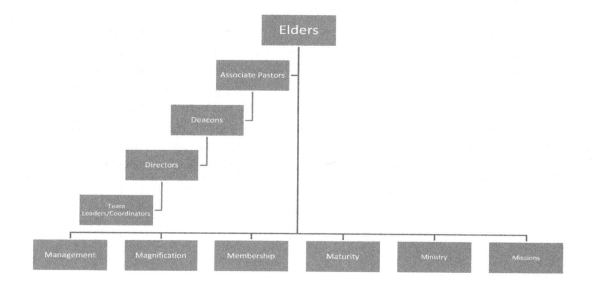

The Essential Process of Assimilation of People
Move People to:

Membership ➡️ **Maturity** ➡️ *Ministry/Missions*

Developing genuine relationships; Committed to being accountable to others within the the local body

Learning and living by the Doctrines, Disciplines, Duties of the Christian faith, Functioning within one's demographic in a godly manner

Serving according to one's spiritual gifts, bearing burdens, meeting needs; Outreaching to the community and abroad with love and message of of Jesus Christ

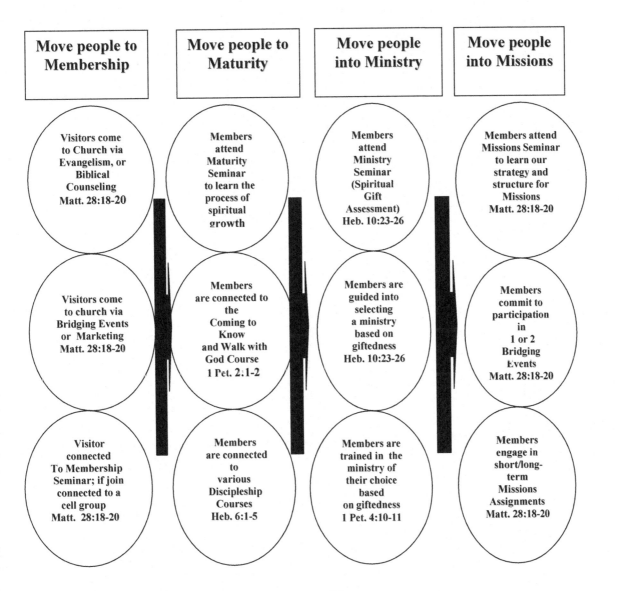

Move people to Membership	Move people to Maturity	Move people into Ministry	Move people into Missions
Visitors come to Church via Evangelism, or Biblical Counseling Matt. 28:18-20	Members attend Maturity Seminar to learn the process of spiritual growth	Members attend Ministry Seminar (Spiritual Gift Assessment) Heb. 10:23-26	Members attend Missions Seminar to learn our strategy and structure for Missions Matt. 28:18-20
Visitors come to church via Bridging Events or Marketing Matt. 28:18-20	Members are connected to the Coming to Know and Walk with God Course 1 Pet. 2:1-2	Members are guided into selecting a ministry based on giftedness Heb. 10:23-26	Members commit to participation in 1 or 2 Bridging Events Matt. 28:18-20
Visitor connected To Membership Seminar; if join connected to a cell group Matt. 28:18-20	Members are connected to various Discipleship Courses Heb. 6:1-5	Members are trained in the ministry of their choice based on giftedness 1 Pet. 4:10-11	Members engage in short/long-term Missions Assignments Matt. 28:18-20

The Essential Ministries for Discipleship and Evangelism

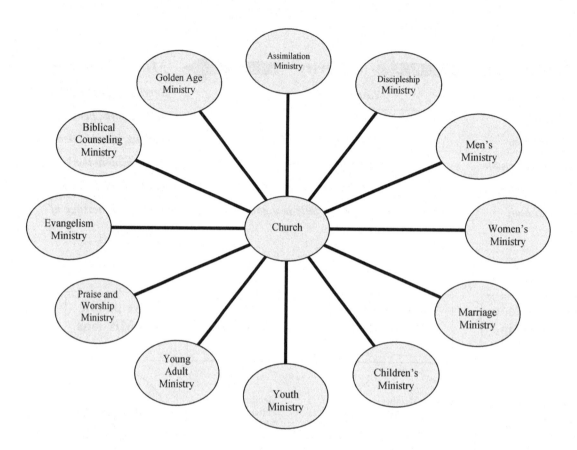

Assimilation Ministry

Purpose: To connect members of the Body to the life of the Church for their spiritual growth and edification

Biblical Imperatives
1. Ephesians 4:11-17
2. Matthew 28:18-20
3. Hebrews 10:24-25
4. Hebrews 3:12-13
5. 2 Corinthians 5:19-21

Objectives:
1. To connect potential members to membership in the Church
2. To connect members to discipleship courses that will lead them into spiritual maturity
3. To connect members to ministries by which they are spiritually gifted to serve in
4. To connect members to outreach and evangelism projects that are sponsored by the Church so that they may share they faith with others accordingly

Process:
1. The Gospel greeters will keep tabs on all visitors and potential members.
2. Those visitors who decide they want to join the Church will lead to the membership seminar where the Seminar leaders will teach them the basic purpose, objectives, process and structure of the Church.
3. Those who are interested in joining will meet with the Elders for a final meeting and then be recognized before the congregation as new members.
4. These new members will be connected to various small groups in the Church according to their demographic for nurture, support and to build edifying relationships.
5. These members will be directed to the maturity seminar whereby they will learn the process of growth and change. This seminar will lead them into the discipleship program of the Church whereby they will be discipled according the curriculum that has been organized for them.
6. These members will be directed to the ministry seminar whereby they will learn the doctrines of spiritual gifts, take a spiritual gift assessment and be guided into a ministry that they are spiritually gifted to serve in.
7. These members will be directed to the mission seminar whereby they will learn about our missionaries and our plans for missions, outreach and evangelism. They

will be asked to participate in at least two outreach and evangelistic activities a year as well as consider taking a short term or long term mission assignment.

8. The process will be monitored by various leaders to make sure that each person in the Church has been connected to membership, maturity, ministry and missions.

9. If there is a problem the Elders will be informed and will address the matter accordingly.

Measurable Goals for the Assimilation Ministry:
1. How many people have we assimilated into membership?
2. How many people have we assimilated into our discipleship program?
3. How many people have we assimilated into ministry service?
4. How many people have we assimilated into missions?
5. How many people in our Church are not connected to any of these areas and why?

Discipleship Ministry

Purpose:
To make disciples of Jesus Christ

Biblical Imperatives:
1. Matthew 28:18-20
2. 2 Timothy 3:16-17
3. 2 Timothy 2:15
4. Colossians 1:27-29
5. 1 Timothy 4:1-5

Objectives:
1. To teach the basic Doctrines of the Christian Faith
2. To teach the basic Disciplines of the Christian Faith
3. To teach the basic Duties of the Christian Faith
4. To teach people how to function as God designed according their demographic in life
5. To equip and train Elders, Pastors, Deacons, Directors, and Team leaders, in leadership God's way
6. To train and equip teachers and small group leaders for all levels of teaching and small Groups
7. To host and provide various workshops, seminars, and trainings that will help develop Church in Spiritual Maturity
8. To educate and develop God's people in such a manner that they function as God intended and develop others to do the same

Process
1. Various courses will be held throughout the week and weekend for all age levels in the doctrines, disciplines and duties of the Christian Faith. There will also be various courses held according the basic demographics of life. (Marriage, single, men, Women, senior citizen, divorced, remarried, pre-married etc.).
2. Listings for available courses will be made available via website, bulletins, mail outs, etc.
3. All who want to take courses will be able to sign up for the course and purchase their materials at the Church.
4. All who are potential leaders will be directed to sign up for various leadership training courses according to the area of leadership they potentially may be serving in.

5. All potential teachers will be directed to sign up for various courses according to their area of teaching.

6. New Members will be lead to the new members track which will entail required and recommended courses for new members to take.

7. The ministry will provide Small Group Discipleship Classes (Sunday School Classes) according to theses basic demographics: (we will develop as many small group classes as needed in these areas):
   a. Golden Age Class (Senior Citizen)
   b. Men's Class
   c. Women's Class
   d. Marriage Class
   e. Young Adult Class
   f. College/Career Age Class
   g. Youth Class
   h. Middle School Class
   i. Children Class
   j. Nursery Class

8. Various workshops and seminars will be provided according to the need and the demographic.

9. A basic discipleship track will be developed for members to follow with various certificates provided upon completion of various discipleship tracks.

10. Missionary training and ministry skill training will be provided according to the need.

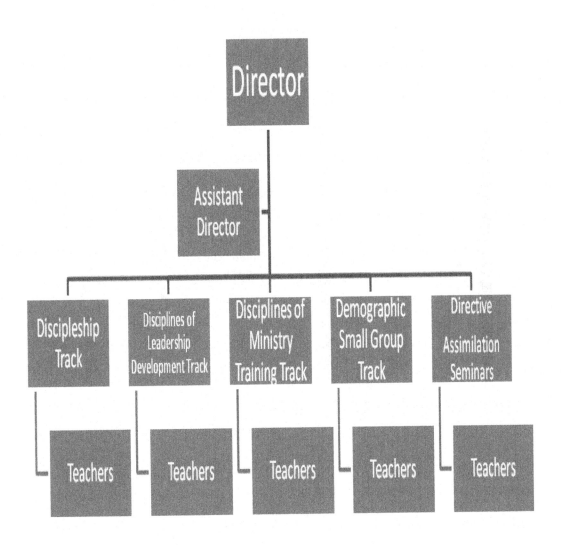

The Essential Plan of Discipleship for the Church

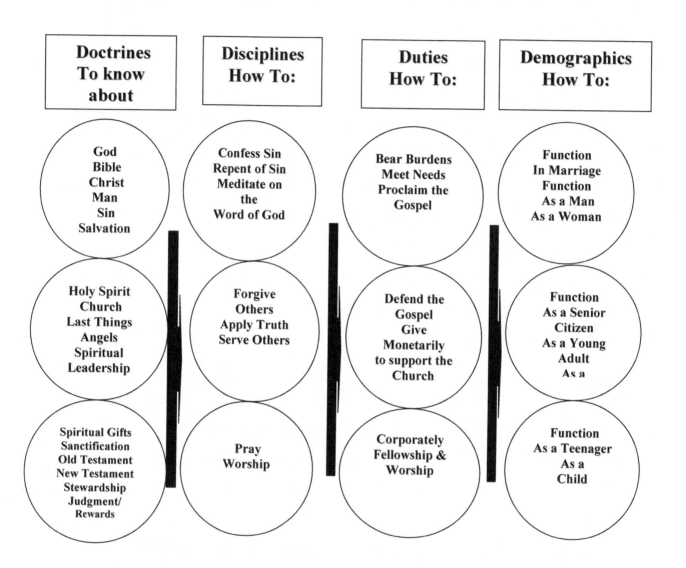

Doctrines To know about

- God
- Bible
- Christ
- Man
- Sin
- Salvation

- Holy Spirit
- Church
- Last Things
- Angels
- Spiritual Leadership

- Spiritual Gifts
- Sanctification
- Old Testament
- New Testament
- Stewardship
- Judgment/ Rewards

Disciplines How To:

- Confess Sin
- Repent of Sin
- Meditate on the Word of God

- Forgive Others
- Apply Truth
- Serve Others

- Pray
- Worship

Duties How To:

- Bear Burdens
- Meet Needs
- Proclaim the Gospel

- Defend the Gospel
- Give Monetarily to support the Church

- Corporately Fellowship & Worship

Demographics How To:

- Function In Marriage
- Function As a Man
- As a Woman

- Function As a Senior Citizen
- As a Young Adult
- As a

- Function As a Teenager
- As a Child

The Essential Discipleship Track

Discovering the Fundamentals of Your Walk with God Track

100   Coming to Know and Walk With God by Nicolas Ellen

101   Dispenstationalism by Charles Ryie

102   Created for God's Glory by Jim Berg

103   Step by Step Through The Old Testament by Waylon Bailey & Tom Hudson

Developing in Your Walk With God Track

104   How People Change (Workbook) by Paul Tripp

105   Step By Step Through the New Testament by Thomas Lea & Tom Hudson

106   Changed Into His Image by Jim Berg

107   Basic Theology by Charles Ryie (The Doctrine of God, Christ, Holy Spirit, Bible)

Deepening your Walk with God Track

108   Pursuing Godliness through the Disciplines of the Christian Faith by Nicolas Ellen

109   Basic Theology by Charles Ryie (The Doctrine of Man, Sin, Salvation, Church)

110   Understanding and Developing a Christ Centered Life and Christ Centered Relationships by Nicolas Ellen

111   Grasping God's Word by J. Scott Duvall/J. Daniel Hays (How to study the Bible curriculum)

Discerning How to Live for God in this World Track

112   Understanding and Developing a Biblical View of Life by Nicolas Ellen

113   Decision Making in the Will of God by Gary Friesen

114   Basic Theology by Charles Ryie (The Doctrine of Angels, Demons, Last Things)

115   What a Way To Live by Tony Evans

Dealing with Your Relationship With Others Track

116   Relationships a Mess Worth Making by Paul Tripp

117   Helping People Change (Workbook) by Paul Tripp

118   Resolving Conflict God's Way by Jim Morris

119   Love the Answer by Rich Thomson

Denouncing the Works of the Flesh

120   <u>With All Your Heart: Identifying and Dealing With Idolatrous Lust</u> by Nicolas Ellen

121   <u>Overcoming Sin and Temptation</u> by John Owen, Kelly M. Kapic, Justin Taylor, John Piper

122   <u>The Purifying Power of Living by Faith in Future Grace</u> by John Piper

123   <u>Essential Virtues: Marks of the Christ-Centered Life</u> by Jim Berg

Disciplines of Ministry and Leadership Training

124   Elder Training Program

125   Pastoral Leadership Training Program

126   Deacon Training Program

127   Director of Ministry Training Program

128   Team Leader Training Program

129   Small Group Leader Training Program

130   Teacher Training Program

131   Biblical Counseling Training Program

132   Missions Training Program

133   Evangelism/Apologetics Training Program

134   Church Planting Training Program

135   Pre-Marital Discipleship Training Program

136   Apartment Ministry Training Program

Demographic Small Group Classes

Golden Age Class(Senior Citizens)

Men's Class

Women's Class

Marriage Class

Young Adult Class

College/Career Age Class

Youth Class

Middle School Class

Children's Class

Nursery Class

Directive Assimilation Seminars

Membership Seminar- all persons interested in becoming a member of the Church will be directed to the Membership Seminar. If they agree with Church – By laws, vision, direction and doctrine of the Church they will sign a Membership Covenant and become members if approved by Elders. They will then be placed in a small group according to their demographic

Maturity Seminar- all who become members must attend the Maturity Seminar whereby they will learn the process of spiritual growth ,the process of biblical change, God's instruction about love and our process of discipleship. If they agree to our process they sign a Maturity Covenant which affirms their willingness to be a disciple and take courses accordingly

Ministry Seminar- all who become members must attend the Ministry Seminar whereby they will learn the Doctrine of Spiritual Gifts and the importance of serving in a ministry according to their gifts. Afterwards, each person will take a spiritual gift assessment to help them to determine where they are gifted. Then they will sign a Ministry Covenant which affirms their commitment to use their gifts to serve others in the Body and abroad. Afterwards they will be guided into to selecting a ministry to serve in according to their giftedness, passion, and time constraints.

Missions Seminar- all who become members must attend the Missions Seminar whereby they will learn our strategy and structure for reaching out to save the lost and provide benefits to the poor and needy outside the Church. They will then be challenged to join our efforts to reach out. They then will sign a Missions Covenant which affirms their commitment to join us in reaching out to the lost. Afterwards, they will select at least 4 events they will participate in for that year and continue to sign up for at least two a year as part of their commitment to the Church

Marriage Ministry

Purpose: To disciple saved married couples to evangelize unsaved married couples

Biblical Imperatives
1. Ephesians 5:22-33
2. Genesis 3:18-25
3. Hebrews 13:4
4. 1Corinthians 13:3-7
5. Matthew 19: 1-12
6. 1Corinthians 7: 1-16
7. 2 Corinthians 5:19-21
8. Ephesians 4: 11-17

Objectives:

1. To build **_Membership_** within the group of married couples—connecting married couples in such a way that genuine relationships can be developed so that accountability, spiritual maturity, and godly friendships can be built with fellow members of the body of Christ on a committed/consistent basis (Hebrews 10:23-24, Romans 12:9-10).

2. To develop **_Magnification_** of the Lord within the group of married couples—establishing a High view of God (Understanding who He is how He operates what He expects and desires of us) and worshipping Him accordingly (John 4:21-24).

3. To develop **_Maturity_** in the Lord within the group of married couples—proper teaching and studying of the Word of God that will lead to spiritual maturity within the group of married couples. This will result in marriages operating according to God's design(Acts 2:42, 2Timothy 4:1-3, Ephesians 4:11-16).

4. To do **_Ministry_** for the Lord within the group of married couples—using our spiritual gifts to bear burdens, meet needs and serve others in tangible manners within the group of married couples and Body of Christ; providing biblical counseling and support where needed (Romans 12:3-8, 1Peter 4:10-11).

5. To do **_Missions_** for the Lord through the group—proper preaching and teaching of the Gospel message to the community, the city, the state, the country and the world in order to make Disciples for Jesus Christ (2 Corinthians 5:18-20, Matthew 28:18-20).

Process:

1. Membership Coordinator and assistants will obtain information about married couples entering the Church.

2. Membership Coordinator and assistants will call couples and welcome them into the Church Body and share pertinent information about the marriage ministry.

3. Membership coordinator and assistants will meet with new members and get them connected with the rest of the couples in this ministry and make sure they are connected to the various activities provided for married couples within the ministry.

4. Ministry Coordinator and assistants will identify the needs of and burdens of these couples so that the Marriage Ministry can effectively serve them.

5. Ministry Coordinator and assistants will make sure these couples discover and use their spiritual gifts and talents to serve their family, the church body, the community and all others places accordingly.

6. Maturity coordinator and assistants will be direct couples into participation in the discipleship and fellowship service that happens outside of Sunday Discipleship so that they may be trained in how function as God designed within their roles and responsibilities as husband and wife.

7. Magnification coordinator and assistants will guide couples into sincere and genuine worship of God in the discipleship and fellowship service.

8. Mission Coordinator and assistants will train couples on how to share and defend their faith in Jesus Christ as they go bear burdens, meet needs and share the Gospel with unbelieving married couples in various areas of the community.

Measurable Goals for the Marriage Ministry:

1. How many married couples have we shared the Gospel with?
2. What needs have we met what burdens have we bared with specific married couples?
3. How many married couples have become Christians as result of this ministry?
4. How many husbands and wives have we equipped to function according to God's design?
5. How many couples are serving according their Spiritual Gifts as a result of this ministry?
6. What truths are we specifically teaching the couples?
7. How many husbands and wives are participating in genuine worship of God?
8. How many relationships have developed as a result of our fellowship?

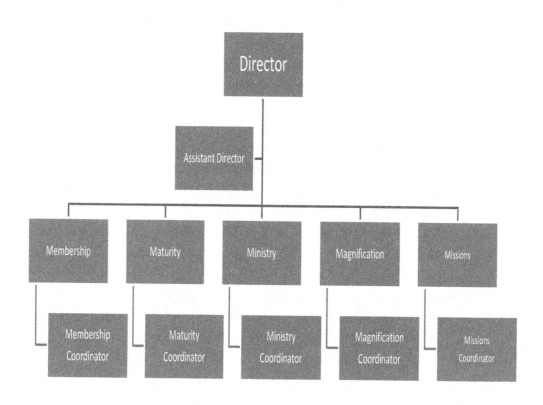

Men's Ministry

Purpose:
To disciple saved men and evangelize unsaved men

Biblical Imperatives:
1. 2 Timothy 2:1-2
2. 1Corinthians 16:13-14
3. Colossians 1:28
4. Matthew 28:18-20
5. 2 Corinthians 5:19-21
6. Ephesians 4:11-17

Objectives:

1. To build ***Membership*** within the group of men—connecting men in such a way that genuine relationships can be developed so that accountability, spiritual maturity, and godly friendships can be built with fellow members of the body of Christ on a committed/consistent basis (Hebrews 10:23-24, Romans 12:9-10).

2. To develop ***Magnification*** of the Lord within the group of men—establishing a High view of God (Understanding who He is how He operates what He expects and desires of us) and Worshipping Him accordingly (John 4:21-24).

3. To develop ***Maturity*** in the Lord within the group of men—proper teaching and studying of the Word of God that will lead to spiritual maturity within the group of men. This will result in men operating in life, with family, and community according to his God given design (Acts 2:42, 2Timothy 4:1-3, Ephesians 4:11-16).

4. To do ***Ministry*** for the Lord within the group of men—using our spiritual gifts to bear burdens, meet needs and serve others in tangible manners within the group of men and Body of Christ (Romans 12:3-8, 1Peter 4:10-11).

5. To do ***Missions*** for the Lord through the group—proper preaching and teaching of the Gospel message to the community, the city, the state, the country and the world in order to make Disciples for Jesus Christ (2 Corinthians 5:18-20, Matthew 28:18-20).

Process:

1. Membership Coordinator and assistants will obtain information about men entering the Church.
2. Membership Coordinator and assistants will call men and welcome them into the Church Body and share pertinent information about the men's ministry.
3. Membership coordinator and assistants will meet with new members and get them connected with the rest of the men in this ministry and make sure they are connected to the various activities provided for men within the ministry.
4. Ministry Coordinator and assistants will identify the needs of and burdens of these men so that the men's Ministry can effectively serve them.
5. Ministry Coordinator and assistants will make sure these men discover and use their spiritual gifts and talents to serve their family, the church body, the community and all others places accordingly.
6. Maturity coordinator and assistants will be direct men into participation in the weekly discipleship and fellowship service that happens outside of Sunday Discipleship so that they may be trained in how function as God designed within their roles and responsibilities as men; They will be trained in how to disciple family and other men accordingly.
7. Magnification coordinator and assistants will guide men into sincere and genuine worship of God on weekly basis in the weekly discipleship and fellowship service.
8. Mission Coordinator and assistants will train men on how to share and defend their faith in Jesus Christ as they go bear burdens, meet needs and share the Gospel with unbelieving men in various area of the community.

Measurable Goals for the Men's Ministry:

1. How many men have we shared the Gospel with?
2. What needs have we met what burdens have we bared with specific men?
3. How many men have become Christians as result of this   ministry?
4. How many men have we equipped to function according to God's design?
5. How many men are serving according their Spiritual Gifts as a result of this ministry?
6. What truths are we specifically teaching the men?
7. How many men are participating in genuine worship of God?
8. How many relationships have developed as a result of our fellowship?

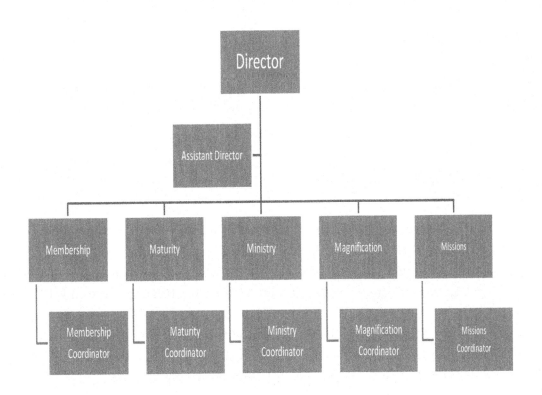

Women's Ministry

Purpose:
To disciple saved women and to evangelize unsaved women

Biblical Imperatives:
1. Titus 2:3-5
2. Romans 6: 1-19
3. Mathew 28:18-20
4. 2 Corinthians 5:19-20
5. Ephesians 4:11-17

Objectives:

1. To build ***Membership*** within the group of women—connecting women in such a way that genuine relationships can be developed so that accountability, spiritual maturity, and godly friendships can be built with fellow members of the body of Christ on a committed/consistent basis (Hebrews 10:23-24, Romans 12:9-10).

2. To develop ***Magnification*** of the Lord within the group of women—establishing a High view of God (Understanding who He is how He operates what He expects and desires of us) and Worshipping Him accordingly (John 4:21-24).

3. To develop ***Maturity*** in the Lord within the group of women—proper teaching and studying of the Word of God that will lead to spiritual maturity within the group of women. This will result in women operating in life, with family, and community according to her God given design (Acts 2:42, 2Timothy 4:1-3, Ephesians 4:11-16).

4. To do ***Ministry*** for the Lord within the group of women—using our spiritual gifts to bear burdens, meet needs and serve others in tangible manners within the group of women and Body of Christ (Romans 12:3-8, 1Peter 4:10-11).

5. To do ***Missions*** for the Lord through the group—proper preaching and teaching of the Gospel message to the community, the city, the state, the country and the world in order to make Disciples for Jesus Christ (2 Corinthians 5:18-20, Matthew 28:18-20).

Process:

1. Membership Coordinator and assistants will obtain information about women entering the Church.
2. Membership Coordinator and assistants will call women and welcome them into the Church Body and share pertinent information about the Women's Ministry.
3. Membership coordinator and assistants will meet with new members and get them connected with the rest of the women in this ministry and make sure they are connected to the various activities provided for women within the ministry.
4. Ministry Coordinator and assistants will identify the needs of and burdens of these women so that the Women's Ministry can effectively serve them.
5. Ministry Coordinator and assistants will make sure these women discover and use their spiritual gifts and talents to serve their family, the church body, the community and all others places accordingly.
6. Maturity coordinator and assistants will be direct women into participation in the weekly discipleship and fellowship service that happens outside of Sunday Discipleship so that they may be trained in how to function as God designed within their roles and responsibilities as women.
7. Magnification coordinator and assistants will guide women into sincere and genuine worship of God on weekly basis in the weekly discipleship and fellowship service.
8. Mission Coordinator and assistants will train women on how to share and defend their faith in Jesus Christ as they go bear burdens, meet needs and share the Gospel with unbelieving women in various areas of the community.

Measurable Goals for the Women's Ministry:

1. How many women have we shared the Gospel with?
2. What needs have we met what burdens have we bared with specific women?
3. How many women have become Christians as result of this ministry?
4. How many women have we equipped to function according to God's design?
5. How many women are serving according their Spiritual Gifts as a result of this ministry?
6. What truths are we specifically teaching the women?
7. How many women are participating in genuine worship of God?
8. How many relationships have developed as a result of our fellowship?

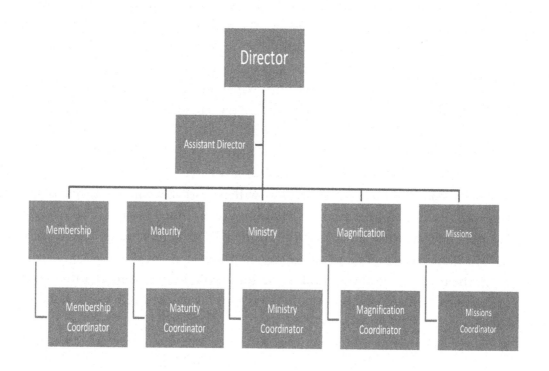

Golden Age Ministry

Purpose:
To disciple saved Senior Citizens and to evangelize unsaved Senior Citizens

Biblical Imperatives:
1. Acts 6:1-6
2. 1Timothy 5:1-16
3. Romans 6: 1-19
4. Mathew 28:18-20
5. 2Corinthians 5:19-20
6. Ephesians 4:11-17

Objectives:

1. To build ***Membership*** within the group of Senior Citizens—connecting Senior Citizens in such a way that genuine relationships can be developed so that accountability, spiritual maturity, and godly friendships can be built with fellow members of the body of Christ on a committed/consistent basis (Hebrews 10:23-24, Romans 12:9-10).

2. To develop ***Magnification*** of the Lord within the group of Senior Citizens—establishing a High view of God (Understanding who He is how He operates what He expects and desires of us) and Worshipping Him accordingly (John 4:21-24).

3. To develop ***Maturity*** in the Lord within the group of Senior Citizens—proper teaching and studying of the Word of God that will lead to spiritual maturity within the group of Senior Citizens. This will result in Senior Citizens operating in life, with family, and community according to his/her God given design(Acts 2:42, 2 Timothy 4:1-3, Ephesians 4:11-16).

4. To do ***Ministry*** for the Lord within the group of women—using spiritual gifts to bear burdens, meet needs and serve others in tangible manners within the group of Senior Citizens and Body of Christ (Romans 12:3-8, 1Peter 4:10-11).

5. To do ***Missions*** for the Lord through the group—proper preaching and teaching of the Gospel message to the community, the city, the state, the country and the world in order to make Disciples for Jesus Christ (2 Corinthians 5:18-20, Matthew 28:18-20).

Process:

1. Membership Coordinator and assistants will obtain information about Senior Citizens entering the Church.

2. Membership Coordinator and assistants will call Senior Citizens and welcome them into the Church Body and share pertinent information about the Senior Citizen's Ministry.

3. Membership coordinator and assistants will meet with new members and get them connected with the rest of the Senior Citizens in this ministry and make sure they are connected to the various activities provided for Senior Citizens within the ministry.

4. Ministry Coordinator and assistants will identify the needs of and burdens of these Senior Citizens so that the Senior Citizen's Ministry can effectively serve them.

5. Ministry Coordinator and assistants will make sure these Senior Citizens discover and use their spiritual gifts and talents to serve their family, the church body, the community and all others places accordingly.

6. Maturity coordinator and assistants will be direct Senior Citizens into participation into the discipleship and fellowship service that happens outside of Sunday Discipleship so that they may be trained in how to function as God designed within their roles and responsibilities Senior Citizens.

7. Magnification coordinator and assistants will guide Senior Citizens into sincere and genuine worship of God in the discipleship and fellowship service.

8. Mission Coordinator and assistants will train Senior Citizens on how to share and defend their faith in Jesus Christ as they go bear burdens, meet needs and share the Gospel with unbelieving Senior Citizens in various areas of the community.

Measurable Goals for the Women's Ministry:

1. How many Senior Citizens have we shared the Gospel with?

2. What needs have we met what burdens have we bared with specific Senior Citizens?

3. How many Senior Citizens have become Christians as result of this ministry?

4. How many Senior Citizens have we equipped to function according to God's design?

5. How many Senior Citizens are serving according their Spiritual Gifts as a result of this ministry?

6. What truths are we specifically teaching the Senior Citizens?

7. How many Senior Citizens are participating in genuine worship of God?

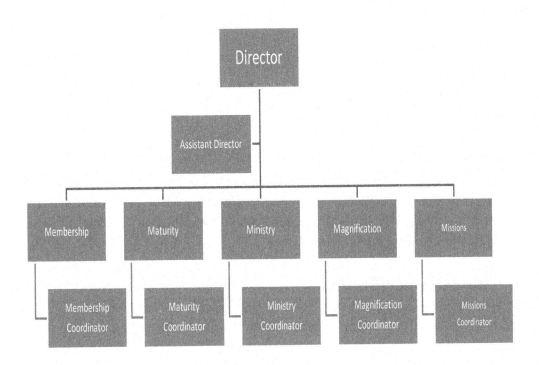

Young Adult Ministry

Purpose: To disciple young adults and evangelize young adults in the college and career demographic

Biblical Imperatives:
1. Titus 2:1-8
2. 1Peter 5:5
3. Matthew 28:18-20
4. 2 Corinthians 5:19-21
5. Ephesians 4:11-17

Objectives:

1. To build ***Membership*** within the group—connecting young adults in such a way that genuine relationships can be developed so that accountability, spiritual maturity, and godly friendships can be built with fellow members of the body of Christ on a committed/consistent basis (Hebrews 10:23-24, Romans 12:9-10).

2. To develop ***Magnification*** of the Lord within the group—establishing a High view of God (Understanding who He is how He operates what He expects and desires of us) and worshipping Him accordingly (John 4:21-24).

3. To develop ***Maturity*** in the Lord within the group—proper teaching and studying of the Word of God that will lead to spiritual maturity within the group (Acts 2:42, 2Timothy 4:1-3, Ephesians 4:11-16).

4. To do ***Ministry*** for the Lord within the group—using our spiritual gifts to bear burdens, meet needs and serve others in tangible manners within the group and Body of Christ (Romans 12:3-8, 1Peter 4:10-11).

5. To do ***Missions*** for the Lord through the group—proper preaching and teaching of the Gospel message to the community, the city, the state, the country and the world in order to make Disciples for Jesus Christ (2 Corinthians 5:18-20, Matthew 28:18-20).

Process:

1. Membership Coordinator and assistants will obtain information about young adults entering the Church.

2. Membership Coordinator and assistants will call young adults and welcome them into the Church Body and share pertinent information about the young adult ministry.

3. Membership coordinator and assistants will meet with new members and get them connected with the rest of the young adults in this ministry and make sure they are connected to the various activities provided for young adults within the ministry.

4. Ministry Coordinator and assistants will identify the needs of and burdens of these young adults so that the Young Adult Ministry can effectively serve them.

5. Ministry Coordinator and assistants will make sure these Young Adults discover and use their spiritual gifts and talents to serve their family, the church body, he community and all others places accordingly.

6. Maturity coordinator and assistants will be direct young adults into participation in the discipleship and fellowship service that happens outside of Sunday Discipleship so that they may be trained in how to function as God designed within their roles and responsibilities as young adults.

7. Magnification coordinator and assistants will guide young adults into sincere and genuine worship of God in the discipleship and fellowship service.

8. Mission Coordinator and assistants will train young adults on how to share and defend their faith in Jesus Christ as they go bear burdens, meet needs and share the Gospel with unbelieving young adults in various area of the community.

Measurable Goals for the Ministry:

1. How many young adults have we shared the Gospel with?

2. What needs have we met what burdens have we bared with specific young adults?

3. How many young adults have become Christians as result of this ministry?

4. How many young adults have we equipped to function according to God's design?

5. How many young adults are serving according their Spiritual Gifts as a result of this ministry?

6. What truths are we specifically teaching the young adults?

7. How many young adults are participating in genuine worship of God?

8. How many relationships have developed as a result of our fellowship?

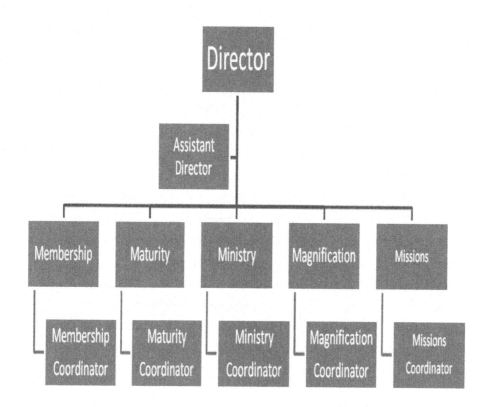

Youth Ministry

Purpose: To disciple saved youth and evangelize unsaved youth

Biblical Imperatives:
1. Ephesians 6: 4
2. Proverbs 22:6
3. Deuteronomy 6:1-9
4. Matthew 28:18-20
5. 2 Corinthians 5:19-21
6. Ephesians 4:11-17

Objectives:

1. To build **_Membership_** within the group of youth—connecting youth in such a way that genuine relationships can be developed so that accountability, spiritual maturity, and godly friendships can be built with fellow members of the body of Christ on a committed/consistent basis (Hebrews 10:23-24, Romans 12:9-10).

2. To develop **_Magnification_** of the Lord within the group of youth—establishing a High view of God (Understanding who He is how He operates what He expects and desires of us) and worshipping Him accordingly (John 4:21-24).

3. To develop **_Maturity_** in the Lord within the group of youth—proper teaching and studying of the Word of God that will lead to spiritual maturity within the group of youth. This will result in youth operating in life, with family, and community according to his/her God given design (Acts 2:42, 2Timothy 4:1-3, Ephesians 4:11-16).

4. To do **_Ministry_** for the Lord within the group of youth—using our spiritual gifts to bear burdens, meet needs and serve others in tangible manners within the group of youth and Body of Christ (Romans 12:3-8, 1Peter 4:10-11).

5. To do **_Missions_** for the Lord through the group—proper preaching and teaching of the Gospel message to the community, the city, the state, the country and the world in order to make Disciples for Jesus Christ (2 Corinthians 5:18-20, Matthew 28:18-20).

Process:

1. Membership Coordinator and assistants will obtain information about youth entering the Church.
2. Membership Coordinator and assistants will call youth and welcome them into the Church Body and share pertinent information about the youth ministry.
3. Membership coordinator and assistants will meet with new members and get them connected with the rest of the youth in this ministry and make sure they are connected to the various activities provided for youth within the ministry.
4. Ministry Coordinator and assistants will identify the needs of and burdens of these youth so that the Youth Ministry can effectively serve them.
5. Ministry Coordinator and assistants will make sure these youth discover and use their spiritual gifts and talents to serve their family, the church body, the community and all others places accordingly.
6. Maturity coordinator and assistants will be direct youth into participation in the Sunday morning discipleship and weekly discipleship so that they may be trained in how to function as God designed.
7. Magnification coordinator and assistants will guide youth into sincere and genuine worship of God on weekly basis in the Sunday Morning and weekly discipleship.
8. Mission Coordinator and assistants will train youth on how to share and defend their faith in Jesus Christ as they go bear burdens, meet needs and share the Gospel with unbelieving youth in various area of the community.

Measurable Goals for the Youth Ministry:

1. How many youth have we shared the Gospel with?
2. What needs have we met what burdens have we bared with specific youth?
3. How many youth have become Christians as result of this ministry?
4. How many youth have we equipped to function according to God's design?
5. How many youth are serving according their Spiritual Gifts as a result of this ministry?
6. What truths are we specifically teaching the youth?
7. How many youth are participating in genuine worship of God?
8. How many relationships have developed as a result of our fellowship?

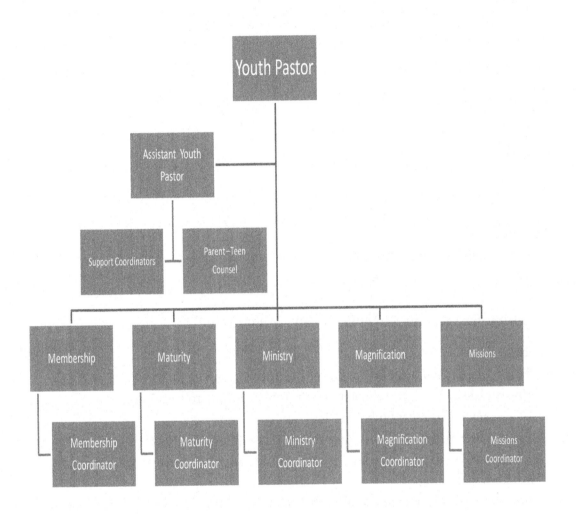

Children's Ministry

Purpose
To evangelize unsaved children and to disciple saved children

Biblical Imperatives:
1. Ephesians 6: 4
2. Proverbs 22:6
3. Deuteronomy 6:1-9
4. Matthew 28:18-20
5. 2 Corinthians 5:19-21
6. Ephesians 4:11-17

Objectives
1. Introduce each child to God.
2. Teach each child to walk like Jesus.
3. Help each child to discover their gifts.
4. Encourage each child to help and love others.

Process
1. Teach about God and Jesus through Sunday School classes
2. Encourage each child to practice what was taught to him/her
3. Love each child for who he/she is
4. Assist each child in discovering their gifts and encourage them to practice them
5. Be sensitive to the burden of each child and help him/her to bring them to the authority of Jesus
6. Remind and encourage the children to share what they learned in class
7. Partner with parents in teaching biblical truth

Measurable Goals for the Children's Ministry:
1. How many children have we shared the Gospel with?
2. What needs have we met what burdens have we bared with specific children?
3. How many children have become Christians as result of this ministry?
4. How many children have we equipped to function according to God's design?
5. How many children are serving according their Spiritual Gifts as a result of this ministry?
6. What truths are we specifically teaching the children?
7. How many children are participating in genuine worship of God?

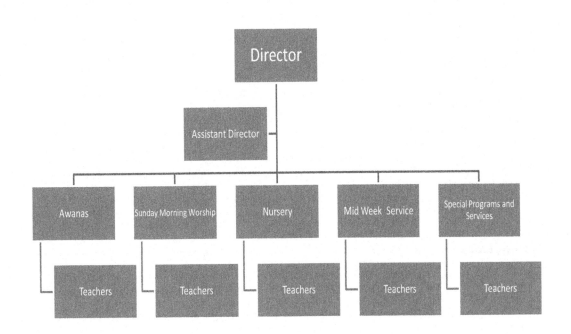

Praise and Worship Ministry

Purpose: To establish an atmosphere through hymns, spiritual songs, and melodies whereby God is worshiped and praised for who He is, how He operates, and what He has done

Biblical Imperatives:
1. John 4:21-24
2. Ephesians 5:18-19
3. Colossians 3:16
4. Psalm 150
5. Psalm 98:5
6. Psalm 147:7
7. Psalm 149:3

Objectives
1. To have the praise team present various songs that leads the Body of Christ into genuine praise of God.
2. To have the praise team present various songs that leads the Body of Christ into genuine worship of God.
3. To provide a mixture of praise and worship songs that will connect with the various people groups within the congregation.
4. To organize and present various praise and worship songs music that fits the message and the moment.

Process:
1. The praise and worship leader will meet with the Pastor to discuss flow and order of service in order to determine the best course of music for the worship service.
2. The praise team will rehearse the songs accordingly in preparation for the service.
3. The praise team will provide songs of praise and songs of worship accordingly to lead the congregation into genuine praise and worship during the worship service.

Measurable Goals for the Praise and Worship Ministry:
1. Are we leading people into genuine worship and praise of God?
2. Are the songs we sing consistent with Word of God?
3. Are the songs we sing supporting the message of the Pastor?

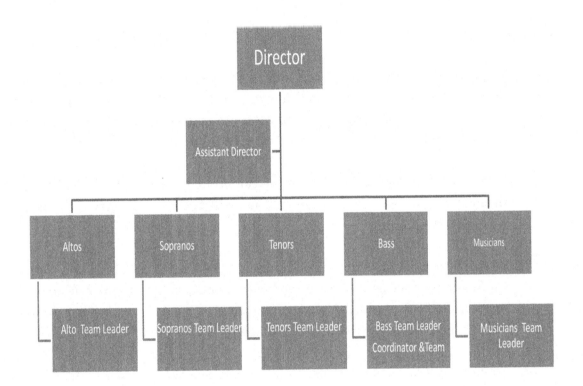

Evangelism Ministry

Purpose: To reach out to various people groups through various means in order to present the Gospel of Jesus Christ anticipating salvation of the unbeliever as God wills

Biblical Imperatives:
1. Matthew 28:18-20
2. 2 Corinthians 5:19-21

Objectives:

1. To provide bridging events/programs to the community – events and activities that build a bridge between the church and the community whereby they know we are in the community to bear burdens and meet needs as a platform to share the Gospel of Jesus resulting in sharing the Gospel of Jesus Christ.

2. To do strategic evangelism- reach the community with the Gospel of Jesus Christ through various modes and media that will best fit the various people groups within the community.

3. To do short term mission trips- to target various areas of the state, country, and world whereby we go in for a period of 6 months or less to provide some form of service that will bear a burden and meet a need as a platform to share the Gospel of Jesus Christ resulting in sharing the Gospel of Jesus Christ.

4. To do long term mission trips- to target various areas of the state, country, and world whereby we go in for a long period of time to provide some form of service that will bear a burden and meet a need as a platform to share the Gospel of Jesus Christ resulting in sharing the Gospel of Jesus Christ.

Process

1. The missions seminar coordinator and team will provide seminars to new members of the church to explain our plans for evangelism through our Missions Seminar.
2. The missions seminar coordinator and team will make sure all members sign up for at least two bridging events of the church to the community at the end of the missions seminar.
3. The bridging event coordinator and team will promote, recruit, and train members to participate in the bridging events that will happen throughout the year.

4. The local evangelism coordinator and team will promote, recruit, and train members to participate in the various modes and media of evangelism that will happen throughout the year.

5. The Short term missions coordinator and team will promote, recruit, and train members for the various short term mission trips that the church will take throughout the year.

6. The long term missions coordinator and team will promote, recruit, and train members for the various long term mission trips that the church will take within the year.

Measurable Goals for the Evangelism Ministry:

1. What communities, cities, states, and countries are we doing evangelism?
2. What burdens, and needs are we meeting in these communities, cities, states, and countries?
3. How many people have we shared the Gospel with?
4. How many people have become Christians as result of this ministry?
5. How many members have we equipped for bridging events, local evangelism, short missions, and long term missions?
6. How many members have we recruited to this ministry?

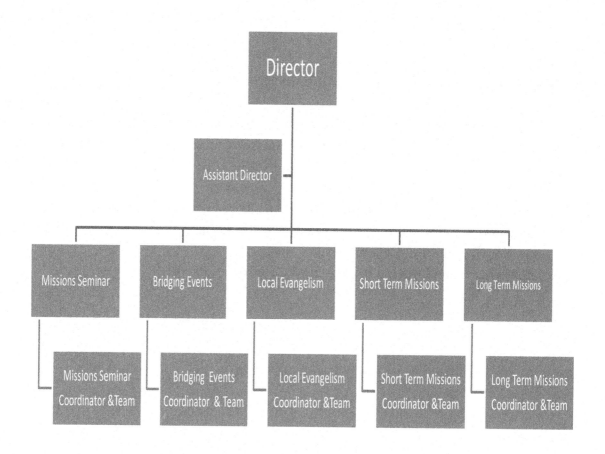

EVERY CHRISTIAN A COUNSELOR
CHAPTER 10
SAMPLE OF STRUCTURED BIBLICAL COUNSELING MINISTRY

As we have stated in the previous chapters, genuine biblical counseling is an avenue whereby evangelism and discipleship takes place on an interpersonal level as the Word of God is used within the context it was written to address the problems and concerns of individuals anticipating the salvation of sinners and the sanctification of Saints, as God wills. Every Christian is called to the work of evangelism and discipleship, which means that every Christian is a biblical counselor! Biblical counseling incorporates the phases of change, the stages of spiritual growth, and the key areas of life where changes take place, into a system to help Christians progress into the sanctification of Jesus Christ. The phases of the change are developed through the stages of spiritual growth. These phases of change and stages of spiritual growth are applied to key areas of life where God holds man accountable to obedience and for disobedience.

There are a few components that help to define the ministry and explain how the ministry should operate. Consider developing a purpose statement, objectives, structure, ministry descriptions, and process within the structure to define the ministry and explain the process of how the biblical counseling ministry should operate within the context of your local congregation. Also consider explaining how the ministry will train and reproduce workers for the ministry. Moreover, consider having a policy for biblical counseling, consent to counsel /release of liability form, personal data inventory form, in-session counseling form, and case report form as tool to help in the procedure of counseling within the ministry. Here are some examples of what this could look like for your ministry.

Biblical Counseling Ministry

Purpose: To assist individuals with various problems and concerns through biblical counseling as well as train, develop and equip people to serve in the biblical counseling ministry according to the Word of God.

Biblical Imperatives:
1. Romans 15:14
2. 2 Timothy 3:16-17
3. 1 Thessalonians 5:14
4. Ephesians 4:1-32
5. 1 Corinthians 13:4-7
6. Matthew 6:33
7. Ephesians 4:17-24
8. Galatians 6:1-3
9. 1 Corinthians 6:1-8
10. Romans 12:1-21

Objectives:
1. To provide pre-marital counseling to all who are seeking to get married in the local Body and the community.
2. To provide biblical answers and solutions to people dealing with marital problems, mental disorders, sexual and substance worship disorder issues, crisis issues, general matters, and parenting problems in the local Body of Christ and the community.
3. To train leaders, laymen, and other churches in the discipline of biblical counseling through various workshops, training courses, videos, and guest lecturers.

Process
1. Members or individuals within the community who are interested in receiving help will call or come by to set up an appointment.
2. Each person will fill out a *consent to counsel* form, release of liability form and a personal data inventory form to determine how the ministry can best serve them.
3. Upon filling out the application each individual or group of individuals will receive a one hour discipleship counseling session to determine how the ministry can best meet their needs.

4. The assimilation counselor will then advise them on who can best serve them within the ministry and connect them to that biblical counselor that can best address their concerns.

5. The assimilation counselor will set up the appointment for the individual or individuals according to a time that works accordingly for all involved.

6. Upon the connection, the biblical counselor will begin the process of helping the individual or individuals via biblical counseling.

7. The ministry will provide a 56 week biblical counseling training course that will be offered to individuals, churches, and organizations and use it as an avenue to lead them into NANC certification.

8. The ministry will train churches and organizations on how to facilitate the training at their locations accordingly.

Measurable Goals for the Ministry:
1. How many individual have we lead to Christ through this ministry?
2. How many individuals have we prepared for marriage through this ministry?
3. How many individual have we protected from marriage through this ministry?
4. How many parents have we helped in their situation?
5. How many marriages have we been able to help function as God intended?
6. How many individuals have we helped to overcome their mental disorders?
7. How many individuals have we helped through a crisis?
8. How many individuals have we helped through substance and sexual worship disorders?
9. How many individual have we helped cope with their general issues?
10. How many have equipped and trained to serve in this counseling ministry and other counseling ministries abroad?

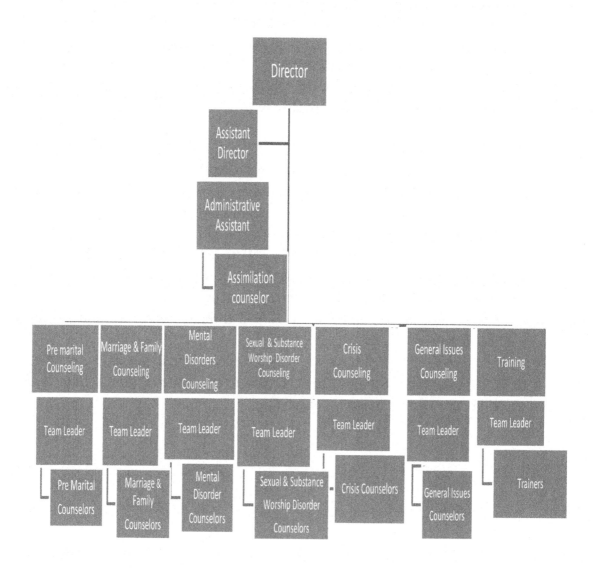

Position Title: Director of Biblical Counseling Ministry

Purpose of the Position: To oversee, manage and develop the biblical counseling ministry

Reports to: Senior Pastor or person he assigns

Responsible for:
- Overseeing and managing the operations of the biblical counseling ministry
- Equipping and training the workers to function as they are gifted to serve in the ministry
- Developing and implementing systems that help the ministry to function efficiently and effectively
- Developing and maintaining policies that will ensure the quality and consistency of the ministry
- Making sure all administrative procedures and policies of the Church are being followed accordingly within the ministry

Primary Strength/Gifts/Talents Required:
- Must be a Christian.
- Must be able to handle difficult people and difficult situations with a positive attitude and appropriate conflict resolution skills.
- Must work well in a team relationship with Church leaders and ministry workers.
- Must be able to build a team that is able to counsel individuals accordingly
- Must have good managerial and people skills or be willing to develop them.
- Must be computer literate or able to learn.
- Must be able to develop programs/systems/courses to equip the couples and those working in the ministry.
- Must be able to network with local para-church organizations.

Measurable Goals for the Position:
- What systems have been implemented that help this ministry function efficiently and effectively as a result of my position?
- How many workers have been recruited and trained to work with the biblical counseling ministry?
- How many individuals have we helped through this ministry?
- What policies and procedures have been implemented or updated as a result of my position?

Position Title: Assistant Director of Biblical Counseling Ministry

Purpose of the Position: To assist the director in overseeing, managing and developing the biblical counseling ministry

Reports to: Director of Biblical Counseling Ministry

Responsible for assisting the director in:
- Overseeing and managing the operations of the biblical counseling ministry.
- Equipping and training the workers to function as they are gifted to serve in the ministry.
- Developing and implementing systems that help the ministry to function efficiently and effectively.
- Developing and maintaining policies that will ensure the quality and consistency of the ministry.
- Making sure all administrative procedures and policies of the Church are being followed accordingly within the ministry.

Primary Strength/Gifts/Talents Required:
- Must be a Christian.
- Must be able to handle difficult people and difficult situations with a positive attitude and appropriate conflict resolution skills.
- Must work well in a team relationship with Church leaders and ministry workers.
- Must be able to build a team that is able to counsel individuals accordingly.
- Must have good managerial and people skills or be willing to develop them.
- Must be computer literate or able to learn.
- Must be able to develop programs/systems/courses to equip the couples and those working in the ministry.
- Must be able to network with local para-church organizations.

Measurable Goals for the Position:
- What systems are have I implemented that help this ministry function efficiently and effectively as a result of my position?
- How many workers have been recruited and trained to work with the biblical counseling ministry?
- How many individuals have we helped through this ministry?
- What policies and procedures have been implemented or updated as a result of my position?

Position Title: Administrative Assistant

Purpose of the Position: To handle all paper work and administrative task that is involved with the ministry and to keep workers and others abreast of meetings and pertinent information.

Reports to: Director of Biblical Counseling Ministry

Responsible For:
- Assisting the Director in the day to day administrative activities of the ministry.
- Setting up and coordinating all trainings, meetings, and events as assigned by the director.
- Setting up and arranging any counseling sessions as assigned by the director.
- Assisting in the planning, coordinating, and implementing of all programs, systems, seminars, courses, policies and procedures.

Primary Strengths/ Gifts/ Talents Required:
- Must be a Christian.
- Must be able to handle difficult people and difficult situations with a positive attitude and appropriate conflict resolution skills.
- Must work well in a team relationship with Church Leaders and ministry workers.
- Must have the gift of administration or serving.
- Must be computer literate or willing to learn.
- Must have good clerical skills or willing to learn.
- Must be able to handle multi-task well.
- Must be able to think wisely and make quick decisions.
- Must have good managerial skills or be ready to learn.

Measurable Goals for the Position:
- In what ways has the ministry been able to function effectively as result of your service?
- What programs, classes, activities, seminars, policies, and procedures were able to be implemented as a result of your service?

Position Title: Assimilation Counselor

Purpose of the Position: To handle all paper work and administrative task that is involved with connecting individuals with the proper counselor to serve them accordingly.

Reports to: Director of Biblical Counseling Ministry

Responsible For:
- Meeting with individuals to determine what counselor is best suited for their problem.
- Providing empathy and sympathy according to the need of moment.
- Providing encouragement and support in the need of the moment.
- Setting up and arranging all counseling sessions accordingly.

Primary Strengths/ Gifts/ Talents Required:
- Must be a Christian.
- Must be able to handle difficult people and difficult situations with a positive attitude and appropriate conflict resolution skills.
- Must work well in a team relationship with Church Leaders and ministry workers.
- Must have the gift of administration or serving or exhortation or compassion.
- Must be computer literate or willing to learn.
- Must have good clerical skills or willing to learn.
- Must be able to handle multi-task well.
- Must be able to think wisely and make quick decisions.
- Must have good managerial skills or be ready to learn.

Measurable Goals for the Position:
- How many individual have been consistently connected to the proper counselor as a result of my work?
- Has the paper work been properly organized and coordinated accordingly?

Position Title: Premarital Counseling Team leader

Purpose of Position: To oversee the biblical counseling and instruction to men and women who are seeking to be married.

Reports to: **Director of Biblical Counseling**

Responsible for Making sure the counselors are:
- Working with Premarital couples through their homework assignments.
- Helping people to determine if marriage is feasible or not according to their spiritual maturity.
- Providing empathy and sympathy according to the need of moment.
- Providing encouragement and support in the need of the moment.
- Exposing the strengths and growth areas of their relationship.
- Exposing character flaws of each person and helping them to deal with those character flaws.
- Identifying sin patterns that need to be put off in each individual.
- Identifying Godly patterns that need to be put on in each individual.
- Helping couples learn how to function according to God's design for marriage.
- Helping couples decide if their decision to get married is a wise or foolish decision.
- Keeping accurate records of the time spent and issues worked on.

Primary Strengths/Gifts/Talents Required:
- Must be a Christian.
- Must be able to handle difficult people and difficult situations with a positive attitude and appropriate conflict resolution skills.
- Must work well in a team relationship with church leaders and ministry workers and have good people skills.
- Must be trained in biblical counseling.
- Must have the gift(s) of serving or compassion or exhortation or teaching.

Measurable Goals for the Position:
- How many couples have we prepared for marriage?
- How many couples have we helped to wait for marriage?
- How many couples have divorced after being trained through this ministry?
- How many couples has become a part of our ministry after going through the process?

Position Title: Premarital Counselor

Purpose of Position: To provide biblical counseling and instruction to men and women who are seeking to be married.

Reports to: Team Leader

Responsible for:
- Working with Premarital couples through their homework assignments.
- Helping people to determine if marriage is feasible or not according to their spiritual maturity.
- Providing empathy and sympathy according to the need of moment.
- Providing encouragement and support in the need of the moment.
- Exposing the strengths and growth areas of their relationship.
- Exposing character flaws of each person and helping them to deal with those character flaws.
- Identifying sin patterns that need to be put off in each individual.
- Identifying Godly patterns that need to be put on in each individual.
- Helping couples learn how to function according to God's design for marriage.
- Helping couples decide if their decision to get married is a wise or foolish decision.
- Keeping accurate records of the time spent and issues worked on.

Primary Strengths/Gifts/Talents Required:
- Must be a Christian.
- Must be able to handle difficult people and difficult situations with a positive attitude and appropriate conflict resolution skills.
- Must work well in a team relationship with church leaders and ministry workers and have good people skills.
- Must be trained in biblical counseling.
- Must have the gift(s) of serving or compassion or exhortation or teaching.

Measurable Goals for the Position:
- How many couples have we prepared for marriage?
- How many couples have we helped to wait for marriage?
- How many couples have divorced after being trained through this ministry?
- How many couples have become a part of our ministry after going through the process?

Position Title: Marital and Family Counseling Team leader

Purpose of Position: To oversee the biblical counsel and instruction to married couples and families dealing with parenting issues.

Reports to: **Director Counseling**

Responsible for making sure the marriage and family counselors are:
- Training couples in the Biblical view of marriage.
- Training coupled in the Biblical view of parenting.
- Providing empathy and sympathy according to the need of moment.
- Providing encouragement and support in the need of the moment.
- Training couples in their roles and responsibilities of marriage.
- Training couples in their roles and responsibilities in parenting.
- Helping couples learn how to function according to God's design in their marriage.
- Helping couples learn how to function according to design in parenting.
- Exposing the strengths and growth areas of their relationship and parenting.
- Exposing character flaws of each person and helping them to deal with those character flaws.
- Identifying sin patterns that need to be put off in each individual.
- Identifying Godly patterns that need to be put on in each individual.
- Keeping accurate records of the time spent and issues worked on.

Primary Strengths/Gifts/Talents Required:
- Must be a Christian.
- Must be able to handle difficult people and difficult situations with a positive attitude and appropriate conflict resolution skills.
- Must work well in a team relationship with church leaders and ministry workers and have good people skills.
- Must be trained in biblical counseling.
- Must have the gift(s) of serving or compassion or exhortation or teaching.

Measurable Goals for the Position:
- How many couples have we helped to function as God designed within their marriage?
- How many parents have we helped to function as God designed?
- How many couples have we saved from divorce through this ministry?
- How many parents have we helped to deal with rebellious children properly?

- How many couples have become a part of our ministry after going through the process?
- How many parents have become a part of our ministry after going through this process

Position Title: Marriage and Family Counselor

Purpose of Position: To provide biblical counsel and instruction to married couples and families dealing with parenting issues.

Reports to: **Team Leader**

Responsible for :
- Training couples in the Biblical view of marriage.
- Training coupled in the Biblical view of parenting.
- Providing empathy and sympathy according to the need of moment.
- Providing encouragement and support in the need of the moment.
- Training couples in their roles and responsibilities of marriage.
- Training couples in their roles and responsibilities in parenting.
- Helping couples learn how to function according to God's design in their marriage.
- Helping couples learn how to function according to design in parenting.
- Exposing the strengths and growth areas of their relationship and parenting.
- Exposing character flaws of each person and helping them to deal with those character flaws.
- Identifying sin patterns that need to be put off in each individual.
- Identifying Godly patterns that need to be put on in each individual.
- Keeping accurate records of the time spent and issues worked on .

Primary Strengths/Gifts/Talents Required:
- Must be a Christian.
- Must be able to handle difficult people and difficult situations with a positive attitude and appropriate conflict resolution skills.
- Must work well in a team relationship with church leaders and ministry workers and have good people skills.
- Must be trained in biblical counseling.
- Must have the gift(s) of serving or compassion or exhortation or teaching.

Measurable Goals for the Position:
- How many couples have we helped to function as God designed within their marriage?
- How many parents have we helped to function as God designed?
- How many couples have we saved from divorce through this ministry?
- How many parents have we helped to deal with rebellious children properly?
- How many couples have become a part of our ministry after going through the process?
- How many parents have become a part of our ministry after going through this process

Position Title: Mental Disorder Counseling Team leader

Purpose of Position: To oversee the biblical counsel and instruction to individuals dealing with various mental disorders issues.

Reports to: **Director of Counseling**

Responsible for making sure the mental disorder counselors are:
- Training individuals in the Biblical view of their mental disorder.
- Providing empathy and sympathy according to the need of moment.
- Providing encouragement and support in the need of the moment.
- Identifying sin patterns that need to be put off in each individual.
- Identifying Godly patterns that need to be put on in each individual.
- Keeping accurate records of the time spent and issues worked on .

Primary Strengths/Gifts/Talents Required:
- Must be a Christian.
- Must be able to handle difficult people and difficult situations with a positive attitude and appropriate conflict resolution skills.
- Must work well in a team relationship with church leaders and ministry workers and have good people skills.
- Must be trained in biblical counseling.
- Must have the gift(s) of serving or compassion or exhortation or teaching.

Measurable Goals for the Position:
- How many individuals have we helped to understand a biblical view of their mental disorder?
- How many individuals have we helped to overcome their mental disorder and function as God designed?
- How many individuals have become a part of our ministry after going the through the process?

Position Title: Mental Disorder Counselor

Purpose of Position: To provide biblical counsel and instruction to individuals dealing with various mental disorders issues.

Reports to: **Team Leader**

Responsible for:
- Training individuals in the Biblical view of their mental disorder.
- Providing empathy and sympathy according to the need of moment.
- Providing encouragement and support in the need of the moment.
- Identifying sin patterns that need to be put off in each individual.
- Identifying Godly patterns that need to be put on in each individual.
- Keeping accurate records of the time spent and issues worked on .

Primary Strengths/Gifts/Talents Required:
- Must be a Christian.
- Must be able to handle difficult people and difficult situations with a positive attitude and appropriate conflict resolution skills.
- Must work well in a team relationship with church leaders and ministry workers and have good people skills.
- Must be trained in biblical counseling.
- Must have the gift(s) of serving or compassion or exhortation or teaching.

Measurable Goals for the Position:
- How many individuals have we helped to understand a biblical view of their mental disorder?
- How many individuals have we helped to overcome their mental disorder and function as God designed?
- How many individuals have become a part of our ministry after going the through the process?

Position Title: Sexual and Substance Worship Disorder Team leader

Purpose of Position: To oversee the biblical counsel and instruction to individuals dealing with sexual and substance worship disorder issues

Reports to: **Director of Counseling**

Responsible for making sure the sexual and substance disorder counselors are:

- Training individuals in the Biblical view of their sexual and substance worship disorder.
- Providing empathy and sympathy according to the need of moment.
- Providing encouragement and support in the need of the moment.
- Identifying sin patterns that need to be put off in each individual.
- Identifying Godly patterns that need to be put on in each individual.
- Keeping accurate records of the time spent and issues worked on

Primary Strengths/Gifts/Talents Required:

- Must be a Christian.
- Must be able to handle difficult people and difficult situations with a positive attitude and appropriate conflict resolution skills.
- Must work well in a team relationship with church leaders and ministry workers and have good people skills.
- Must be trained in biblical counseling.
- Must have the gift(s) of serving or compassion or exhortation or teaching.

Measurable Goals for the Position:

- How many individuals have we helped to understand a biblical view of their sexual and substance worship disorder?
- How many individuals have we helped to overcome their sexual and substance disorder and function as God designed?
- How many individuals have become a part of our ministry after going the through the process?

Position Title: Sexual and Substance Worship Disorder Counselor

Purpose of Position: To provide biblical counsel and instruction to individuals dealing with sexual and substance worship disorder issues.

Reports to: **Team Leader**

Responsible for :
- Training individuals in the Biblical view of their sexual and substance worship disorder.
- Providing empathy and sympathy according to the need of moment.
- Providing encouragement and support in the need of the moment.
- Identifying sin patterns that need to be put off in each individual.
- Identifying Godly patterns that need to be put on in each individual.
- Keeping accurate records of the time spent and issues worked on.

Primary Strengths/Gifts/Talents Required:
- Must be a Christian.
- Must be able to handle difficult people and difficult situations with a positive attitude and appropriate conflict resolution skills.
- Must work well in a team relationship with church leaders and ministry workers and have good people skills.
- Must be trained in biblical counseling.
- Must have the gift(s) of serving or compassion or exhortation or teaching.

Measurable Goals for the Position:
- How many individuals have we helped to understand a biblical view of their sexual and substance worship disorder?
- How many individuals have we helped to overcome their sexual and substance disorder and function as God designed?
- How many individuals have become a part of our ministry after going the through the process?

Position Title: Crisis Counseling Team Leader

Purpose of Position: To oversee the biblical counsel and instruction to individuals dealing with various crisis such as abuse, molestation, rape, suicide, loss of home, loss of loved one.

Reports to: **Director of Counseling**

Responsible for making sure the crisis counselors are:
- Training individuals in the Biblical view of their crisis.
- Providing empathy and sympathy according to the need of moment.
- Providing encouragement and support in the need of the moment.
- Identifying sin patterns that need to be put off in each individual.
- Identifying Godly patterns that need to be put on in each individual.
- Keeping accurate records of the time spent and issues worked on.

Primary Strengths/Gifts/Talents Required:
- Must be a Christian.
- Must be able to handle difficult people and difficult situations with a positive attitude and appropriate conflict resolution skills.
- Must work well in a team relationship with church leaders and ministry workers and have good people skills.
- Must be trained in biblical counseling.
- Must have the gift(s) of serving or compassion or exhortation or teaching.

Measurable Goals for the Position:
- How many individuals have we helped to understand a biblical view of their crisis?
- How many individuals have we helped to overcome their crisis and function as God designed?
- How many individuals have become a part of our ministry after going the through the process?

Position Title: Crisis Counselor

Purpose of Position: To provide biblical counsel and instruction to individuals dealing with various crisis such as abuse, molestation, rape, suicide, loss of home, loss of loved one.

Reports to: **Team Leader**

Responsible for:
- Training individuals in the Biblical view of their crisis.
- Providing empathy and sympathy according to the need of moment.
- Providing encouragement and support in the need of the moment.
- Identifying sin patterns that need to be put off in each individual.
- Identifying Godly patterns that need to be put on in each individual.
- Keeping accurate records of the time spent and issues worked on.

Primary Strengths/Gifts/Talents Required:
- Must be a Christian.
- Must be able to handle difficult people and difficult situations with a positive attitude and appropriate conflict resolution skills.
- Must work well in a team relationship with church leaders and ministry workers and have good people skills.
- Must be trained in biblical counseling.
- Must have the gift(s) of serving or compassion or exhortation or teaching.

Measurable Goals for the Position:
- How many individuals have we helped to understand a biblical view of their crisis?
- How many individuals have we helped to overcome their crisis and function as God designed?
- How many individuals have become a part of our ministry after going the through the process?

Position Title: General Counseling Team Leader

Purpose of Position: To oversee the biblical counsel and instruction to individuals dealing with general matters such as decision making concerns, friendship matters, individual relationship concerns that are not connected to marriage and family.

Reports to: **Director of Counseling**

Responsible for making sure the general counselors are:
- Training individuals in the Biblical view of their situation.
- Helping individual gain biblical view of relationships.
- Providing empathy and sympathy according to the need of moment.
- Providing encouragement and support in the need of the moment.
- Identifying sin patterns that need to be put off in each individual.
- Identifying Godly patterns that need to be put on in each individual.
- Keeping accurate records of the time spent and issues worked on.

Primary Strengths/Gifts/Talents Required:
- Must be a Christian.
- Must be able to handle difficult people and difficult situations with a positive attitude and appropriate conflict resolution skills.
- Must work well in a team relationship with church leaders and ministry workers and have good people skills.
- Must be trained in biblical counseling.
- Must have the gift(s) of serving or compassion or exhortation or teaching.

Measurable Goals for the Position:
- How many individuals have we helped to understand a biblical view of their situation?
- How many individuals have we helped to make good decisions and handle their relationships as God designed?
- How many individuals have become a part of our ministry after going the through the process?

Position Title: General Counselors

Purpose of Position: To provide biblical counsel and instruction to individuals dealing with general matters such as decision making concerns, friendship matters, and individual relationship concerns that are not connected to marriage and family.

Reports to: **Director of Counseling**

Responsible for:
- Training individuals in the Biblical view of their situation.
- Helping individual gain biblical view of relationships.
- Providing empathy and sympathy according to the need of moment.
- Providing encouragement and support in the need of the moment.
- Identifying sin patterns that need to be put off in each individual.
- Identifying Godly patterns that need to be put on in each individual.
- Keeping accurate records of the time spent and issues worked on .

Primary Strengths/Gifts/Talents Required:
- Must be a Christian.
- Must be able to handle difficult people and difficult situations with a positive attitude and appropriate conflict resolution skills.
- Must work well in a team relationship with church leaders and ministry workers and have good people skills.
- Must be trained in biblical counseling.
- Must have the gift(s) of serving or compassion or exhortation or teaching.

Measurable Goals for the Position:
- How many individuals have we helped to understand a biblical view of their situation?
- How many individuals have we helped to make good decisions and handle their relationships as God designed?
- How many individuals have become a part of our ministry after going the through the process?

Position Title: Biblical Counseling Training Team Leader

Purpose of Position: To oversee biblical counseling training of the church.

<u>Reports to</u>: **Director of Counseling**

Responsible for making sure trainers are:
- Training individuals in the concepts of biblical counseling.
- Training individuals in the mechanics of biblical counseling.
- Training individuals in the apologetics of biblical counseling.
- Training individuals in the history of biblical counseling.
- Identifying sin patterns that need to be put off in each individual.
- Identifying godly patterns that need to be put on in each individual.
- Keeping accurate records of the time spent and issues worked on.

Primary Strengths/Gifts/Talents Required:
- Must be a Christian.
- Must be able to handle difficult people and difficult situations with a positive attitude and appropriate conflict resolution skills.
- Must work well in a team relationship with church leaders and ministry workers and have good people skills.
- Must be trained in biblical counseling.
- Must have the gift(s) of serving or compassion or exhortation or teaching.

Measurable Goals for the Position:
- How many individuals have we trained in biblical counseling?
- How many individuals have become a part of our ministry after going the through the process?

Position Title: Biblical Counseling Trainer

Purpose of Position: To provide biblical counseling training of the church.

<u>Reports to:</u> **Team Leader**

Responsible for:
- Training individuals in the concepts of biblical counseling.
- Training individuals in the mechanics of biblical counseling.
- Training individuals in the apologetics of biblical counseling.
- Training individuals in the history of biblical counseling.
- Identifying sin patterns that need to be put off in each individual.
- Identifying godly patterns that need to be put on in each individual.
- Keeping accurate records of the time spent and issues worked on.

Primary Strengths/Gifts/Talents Required:
- Must be a Christian.
- Must be able to handle difficult people and difficult situations with a positive attitude and appropriate conflict resolution skills.
- Must work well in a team relationship with church leaders and ministry workers and have good people skills.
- Must be trained in biblical counseling.
- Must have the gift(s) of serving or compassion or exhortation or teaching.

Measurable Goals for the Position:
- How many individuals have we trained in biblical counseling?
- How many individuals have become a part of our ministry after going the through the process?

(Example)
A Policy For Biblical Counseling

Are You Interested in Biblical Counseling at _____ Church?

Biblical counselors at _____ are available for a limited number of counseling cases. Our counselors (by design) are not certified by the State of _____; however, each counselor is trained and supervised by other counselors. Additionally, _____ counselors have had extensive training in biblical discipleship counseling and must meet various training requirements established by the Bible and the Director of the Ministry.

Director of the Counseling Ministry
Pastor _____, the director of the Ministry, teaches counseling at _____.
He received his _____ from_____.

The Role of Scripture to the Counselor
If you seek counseling from _____, we want you to know that all counseling will be conducted in accordance with the counselor's understanding of the Scriptures. All counseling will be biblically based, meaning that the Scriptures will be the authority in all cases. _____ Church does **not** subscribe to the teachings and methods of modern psychology or psychiatry, whether expressly secular or any attempted integration with biblical principles. Our counselors are not trained or licensed as psychotherapists or mental health professionals nor do they follow the methods of such persons. Also, our policy is to **not** make referrals to such persons.

If you (the counselee) are not sure that you will be interested in biblically-based counseling, counselee may first attend one or two sessions to discover what biblical discipleship counseling is like. If you or the counselor determines that you (the counselee) are unwilling to use the Bible as the final authority for your life, future counseling sessions will be terminated.

Additionally, each counseling session will conclude with the counselor assigning homework. If counselee is unwilling to complete the assigned homework, future counseling sessions will be terminated until the assigned homework has been completed to the satisfaction of the counselor. Any future sessions can be terminated by either party. However, if you (the counselee) are a member of _____ Church, the Pastor and/or Elders will be notified of the reasons for termination of your counseling sessions and all By-Laws and/or policies of COFBC shall apply. If you are not a member of _____ Church, please note that written correspondence will be sent to your church notifying them of the termination of your counseling sessions and the reasons for said termination.

Non-members of _____Church

Please note that _____ Church is committed to the spiritual health of its members thus, counseling of _____ Church members always takes precedence over all non-member related counseling services.

If counselee is a member in good standing with a church other than _____ Church, counselee is required to invite their Senior Pastor or an Elder to accompany them to the counseling sessions. **It is our first choice that your Senior Pastor/Elder from your local church or one of those in its leadership accompanies counselee to their counseling sessions.** However, if the Senior Pastor or an Elder is unavailable, the counselee must invite someone else in a leadership position from their local church.

We recognize and respect the authority and the discipline of counselee's church. If no one in a leadership position is available to attend counseling sessions with counselee, _____ Church's counselor, based solely on counselor's discernment of the matter, may decide to move forward with counselee. However, counselee **must** provide written permission from their Senior Pastor and/or Elder(s) to attend counseling at _____ Church. Counselee must submit to _____ Church a letter from their leadership (Pastor, Elders, or Deacons) stating that they are aware that counselee is receiving counseling from an outside source and that they approve of _____ Church counseling you – this letter must be signed and on the letterhead of counselee's church. In this letter counselee must also provide _____ Church with the name of a person in their church that will be their accountability partner and a phone number where _____Church can contact this person. We do this because we firmly believe in the leadership of your church and we only want to come along side of them to offer assistance. Also, this will make transfer back to the pastoral care of counselee's church much easier to effect.

Additionally if counselee is unable to bring someone in leadership with them, or provide some form of accountability from their local congregation, _____ Church will not be able to facilitate the counseling process. This is due to the fact that _____Church believes that the Senior Pastor/Elders are responsible for the spiritual well being of their local congregation. Without the involvement or support of the Senior Pastor/Elders or someone in leadership from counselee's church, _____Church would be assuming responsibility for counselee's spiritual well being. _____Church is not willing or biblically able to assume such a responsibility without the permission of counselee's church leadership.

Non-member of a Church

If counselee is currently not a member of a church or not a member in good standing with a church, _____Church will expect counselee to attend their Church on a weekly basis while going through the counseling ministry. For example, if counselee is going to have 13 counseling sessions then _____ Church would expect that counselee would attend the church for 13 weeks. After such time _____ Church will be happy to assist counselee in finding a church home and of course, counselee is welcome to examine _____ Church as a possibility.

Our experience has been that for changes in people to be lasting, people need more than the help they receive in formal counseling. They need the total ministry of a church in which the preaching, teaching and fellowship are providing the same kind of help that is given in the counseling sessions. If counselee does not attend _____ Church on a regular basis (Sunday and Wednesday services at least three (3) times a month) all future counseling sessions will be terminated.

Confidentiality
Absolute confidentiality is not scriptural. In certain circumstances the Bible requires that facts be disclosed to select others (Matt. 18:15ff). In these areas we will follow the policy and procedures of _____ Church. When your church leadership inquires about the status of your sessions, we will disclose to them the information that is necessary for them to effectively and biblically fulfill their responsibility to shepherd you.

BY LAW, there are certain situations in which information about individuals undergoing counseling may be released with or without their permission. These situations are as follows: (Romans 13:1-3)
1. Where it is proven that children are physically abused, neglected, or sexually abused.
2. In emergency situations where there may be proven danger to the counselee or others, as with homicide or suicide, confidentiality may be broken.
3. If a court of law issues a legitimate subpoena relating to a child abuse case, we are required by law to provide the information specifically described in the subpoena.
4. If an unreported life-threatening felony has been committed, we are required by law to report it to the police.

At any time during the counseling, for reasons sufficient to himself/herself, the counselor – as also the counselee -- shall have the option of terminating counseling.

Counseling Fees
_____ Church does not charge a specific fee for counseling. However, since there are costs involved in maintaining this ministry, counselees may want to express their thanks and help to maintain the ministry in a tangible way.

Donations should be made to _____ Church in matters such as these. Also, part of the weekly homework assignments may require counselee to purchase materials related to their counseling process. Counselees are expected to pay for these materials.

Counselee Responsibility
It should be understood that biblical discipleship counseling will involve giving scriptural teaching and making practical application of the same to each individual counselee. Counselee is held fully responsible for how he/she implements that counsel.

Counselors in Training

Here at _____ Church we not only provide biblical discipleship counseling, but are devoted to training biblical counselors. This means that the counselor may have one to two people assisting him/her in each counseling session.

The Bible as the Authority in the Session

We are confident that the Bible has all of the information necessary for life and godliness (2 Pet.1:3). There are no problems between persons or in persons that the Bible fails to address either in general or specific principles. Our counselors are not infallible, nor do they pretend to know all there is to know about biblical teaching and its applications to life, but they are well equipped and competent to help people change. They will make a point to differentiate between God's commands and their suggestions. Counselors will also honestly tell you if they are limited in their capacity to address a matter and will seek help from other trained counselors in matters where they feel it is needed.

Medical/Legal Advice

Please note that_____ Church does **not** give medical or legal advice.

If you are willing to enter into this kind of counseling, please fill out the forms attached below. Once you have filled out the forms please email the forms or mail them to us. (See our contact information.) Once you have emailed or mailed the forms, call us to see when/if scheduled times of counseling are available.

Thank you for your interest in the biblical discipleship counseling ministry of _____ Church.

(Adapted from Wayne Mack at Wayne Mack Ministries)

A Consent to Biblical Counseling
And
Release of Liability Form

What is Expected of You?

It is our belief that change must begin with ourselves as we look to Jesus Christ for the power to change. Therefore, we ask you (counselee) to approach the counseling and encouragement process as an opportunity for personal change and spiritual growth. We ask that you refrain from the temptation of focusing on others, and instead we ask you to focus on what changes God desires to make in your life, in the midst of your circumstances. Be advised that you will be assigned "homework." Homework is a vital part of the change process; therefore, completion of the homework assignments before your next session is expected.

CONFIDENTIALITY CLAUSE

1) Absolute confidentiality is not scriptural. In certain circumstances the Bible requires that facts be disclosed to select others (Matthew 18:15ff). In these areas we follow the guidelines of _____ Church. When your church leadership inquires, we will disclose to them the information they need to effectively and biblically fulfill their responsibility to shepherd you.

2) The privacy and confidentiality of our conversations and records are a privilege of yours and are protected by our ethical principles in all but a few circumstances. BY LAW, there are certain situations in which information about individuals undergoing counseling may be released with or without their permission. These situations are as follows: (Romans 13:1-3)

A. Where it is proven that children are physically abused, neglected, or sexually abused;
B. In emergency situations where it is proven that there may be danger to the counselee or others, as with homicide or suicide, confidentiality may be broken;
C. If a court of law issues a legitimate subpoena relating to a child abuse case, we are required by law to provide the information specifically described in the subpoena;
D. If an unreported life-threatening felony has been committed, we are required by law to report it to the police.

3) We reserve the right to consult with others or appropriate church ministry staff members regarding your sessions. This consultation will be held in the same level of confidence as your sessions. This will involve issues such as:

A. Church discipline matters
B. Seeking wise counsel to help address the matter in a thorough manner
C. Reporting to other leaders on the status of counseling when feasible and appropriate
D. Training of other counselors to learn how to handle cases of the same nature

Resolution of Disagreements

If a dispute should arise between the counselee and the counselor regarding the session or the counselor's advice or conduct, one should bring this dispute to the attention of the Director of the Biblical Discipleship Counseling Ministry of _____ Church. If the dispute cannot be resolved at this level, all parties agree to resolve such dispute by submitting to the Conflict Resolution Team of the Church_____ for full **and** final resolution and conciliation. Both, the counselee and the counselor agree **not** to take this matter to any secular court system. (1 Corinthians 6:1-7)

Waiver of Liability

The undersigned counselee, having sought biblical discipleship counseling as adhered to by _____ Church, a nonprofit religious organization, hereby acknowledges their understanding of the above stated conditions and therefore releases from liability the _____ Church and any/all participating churches, pastors, agents or employees, from a claim or litigation whatsoever arising from the undersigned's participation in the above-mentioned biblical discipleship counseling ministry.

It is further understood, in consideration for receiving any form of counseling from the _____ Church, the person (counselee) receiving the counseling agrees to release and waive any and all claims of any kind against the ministry, the staff, the pastoral/lay counselors or any participating church, which may arise from, result out of, or be related to conduct or advice/counsel given. Additionally, all counsel provided in by _____ Church is provided in accordance with the biblical principles adhered to by the Church and is not necessarily provided in adherence with any local or national psychological or psychiatric association.

That the undersigned agrees that he/she has read and thoroughly understands and agrees to what is expected of them, the confidentiality clause, the resolution of disagreements, _____ Church's policy for counseling that is placed on the website, and the contents of the waiver, and now willingly (without any coercion) consents to and requests said biblical discipleship counseling from _____ Church's biblical discipleship counseling ministry.

SIGNED on this _____ day of _____, AD, 20_____, at

_____.

(County)_____

Signed Name_____

Printed Name_____

Before me, the undersigned authority on this day personally appeared _____, known to me to be the person whose name is subscribed to the foregoing instrument of writing and acknowledged to me that he executed the same for the purposes and consideration thereon expressed. SWORN TO AND SUBSCRIBED BEFORE ME, under my official hand and seal of office this the _____ day of _____, 20_____.

_____
NOTARY PUBLIC In and for the STATE OF TEXAS

Printed Name: _____

My Commission expires: _____

Personal Data Inventory (Here is an example)

Personal Data Inventory
Please complete this inventory carefully

Personal Identification:

Name _____ Birth Date _____

Address_____Zip_____

Age_____ Sex____ Referred By_____

Marital Status:

Single ____ Engaged ____ Married ____ Separated ____ Divorced ____ Widowed ____

Education: (last year completed): _____

Home Phone _____Business Phone _____

Employer _____ Position _____ Years _____

In case of emergency, please contact: _____(name)

_____(Phone numbers)

MARRIAGE AND FAMILY:

Spouse _____Birth Date _____

Age _____ Occupation _____How long employed _____

Home Phone _____Business Phone _____

Date of Marriage _____Length of dating _____

Give brief statement of circumstances of meeting and dating

_____

_____

Have either of you been previously married?_____ To Whom? _____

Have you ever been separated? _____ Filed for divorce? _____

Information about children:

Name	Age	Sex	Living	Yrs.	Ed.	Step-child

Describe relationship to your father _____

Describe relationship to your mother _____

Number of siblings _____Your sibling order _____

Did you live with anyone other than parents? _____

Are your parents living? _____ Do they live locally? _____

143

HEALTH

Describe your health _____

Do you have any chronic conditions? _____ what _____

List important illnesses and injuries or handicaps _____
_____

Date last medical exam _____ Report _____

Physician's name and address _____

Current medication(s) and dosage _____
_____

Have you ever used drugs for other than medical purposes? _____

If yes, please explain _____
_____

Have you ever been arrested? _____

Do you drink alcoholic beverages? _____If so, how frequently and how much
_____

Do you drink coffee? _____ How much _____

Other caffeine drinks? _____ How much _____

Do you smoke? _____ What _____ Frequency _____

Have you ever had interpersonal problems on the job? _____
_____

Have you ever had a severe emotional upset? _____ If yes, explain _____
_____

Have you ever seen a psychiatrist or counselor? _____ If yes, explain _____
_____

Are you willing to sign a release of information form so that your counselor may write
for social, psychiatric, or other medical records?_____

SPIRITUAL:

Denominational preference? _____

Church attending _____

Church attendance per month (circle one)   0   1   2   3   4   5   6   7   8+

Do you believe in God? _____ Do you pray _____

Would you say you are a Christian or still in the process of becoming a Christian
_____

Have you been baptized? _____

How often do you read the Bible? _____ never _____ Occasionally _____ Daily

Explain any recent changes in your religious life_____
_____

WOMEN ONLY:

Have you had any menstrual difficulties? _____ Do you experience tension, tendency to cry, other symptoms prior to your cycle? please explain _____

Is your husband willing to come for counseling? _____

Is he in favor of your coming? _____ If no, explain _____

_____

PROBLEM CHECKLIST:

____ Anger

Anxiety

____ Apathy

____ Appetite

____ Bitterness

____ Change in lifestyle

____ Children

____ Communication

____ Conflict (fights)

____ Deception

____ Decision-making

____ Depression

____ Drunkenness

____ Envy

____ Fear

____ Finances

____ Gluttony

____ Guilt

____ Health

____ Homosexuality

____ Impotence

____ In-laws

____ Loneliness

____ Lust

____ Memory

____ Moodiness

____ Perfectionism

____ Rebellion

____ Sex

____ Sleep

____ Wife Abuse

____ A vice

____ Other

BRIEFLY ANSWER THE FOLLOWING QUESTIONS:

1.   What   is   the   problem   or   concern   that   brings   you   here   today?

_____

_____

_____

_____

_____

2. What have you done about this problem?

_____

_____

_____

_____

_____

_____

3. What are your expectations from counseling?

_____

_____

_____

_____

_____

_____

4. Is there any other information we should know about?

_____

_____

_____

_____

SPIRITUAL CONVICTIONS QUESTIONNAIRE: (Please use the back of this sheet if necessary.)

1. Describe Who God is: _____

_____

2. Describe Who Jesus Christ is: _____

3. Describe the kind of relationship you have with God and His Son Jesus Christ:

_____

_____

4. What is the Definition of a Christian?

_____

_____

5. I am or (I am not) a Christian because:

_____

6. What do you believe about the Bible?

_____

_____

7. What is your definition of sin?

_____

8. What sins do you struggle with the most? _____

9. How do you handle sin in your life?

_____

10. How do you handle guilt?

_____

11. What do you tend to pray about the most?

_____

12. What do you seek to accomplish in life?

_____

13. I do attend or I do not attend church because:

_____

_____

14. I allow Christians or I do not allow Christians to be involved in my life because:

_____

_____

15. The changes I would like make in my life are:

_____

_____

16. What have you learned about yourself and what have you learned about your partner? What changes do you need to make in light of his study:

_____

_____

(Adapted from Wayne Mack & Jay Adams)

In-Session Counseling form (Here is an example)

Step 1 _Connect_ with the Counselee(s): Identify 5 questions you can ask to get to know the counselee(s)

Question 1:

Question 2:

Question 3:

Question 4:

Question 5:

Step 2 _Console_ the Counselee(s): Think through some words of encouragement you can provide within the session:

Step 3 _Collect_ data from the Counselee(s) in regards to their problems and concerns: Identify ten questions you can ask to get to the root of the problem(s) and concern(s)

Question 1:

Question 2:

Question 3:

Question 4:

Question 5:

Question 6:

Question 7:

Question 8:

Question 9:

Question 10:

Step 4 *Categorize* data from the Counselee into Biblical terms and perspectives as you are thinking through Biblical solutions.

    a. As you look at the characteristics of the situation/problem are there any expressions of uncaused fleeing being demonstrated? If so, write them down.

    b. As you look at the characteristics of the situation/problem are there any expressions of uncaused fear being demonstrated? If so, write them down.

    c. As you look at the characteristics of the situation/problem are there any expressions of a sense of guilt being demonstrated? If so, write them down.

    d. As you look at the characteristics of the situation/problem are there any secondary unloving/sinful attitudes, words, actions (unloving /sinful attitudes, words or actions being expressed as a result of the main unloving/sinful attitude, word, or action) being demonstrated? If so, write them down.

Step 5 <u>Communicate</u> to counselee(s) what the Bible defines as the source and the symptoms of the problems in Biblical terms and <u>*clarify*</u> what the Biblical solutions are to those problems.

a. What is the root of the problem (First Level Sin)?

b. What are the byproducts (guilt, au fear, au fleeing, physiological matters, secondary sins ect.) that are occurring as a result the problem?

c. Identify at least Ten Scriptures that can communicate the problem and clarify what the Biblical solutions are for this particular problem.

d. Identify what are key biblical concepts you need to teach in this session to communicate the problem and to clarify the solution.

Concept 1:

Concept 2:

Concept 3:

Concept 4:

Step 6 _**Challenge**_ the Counselee to a commitment to confess, repent, and replace sin with love for God and others. Think through some words of challenge for this particular session:

Step 7 _Construct_ homework for the counselee(s) to apply to their lives that will lead them into confession, repentance, and replacement of sin with love for God and others: Identify what will fit for this closing session:

   a. _**Hope Homework**_ –

   b. _**Doctrinal Homework**_ –

   c. _**Awareness Homework**_ –

   d. _**Embracing God Homework**_ –

   e. _**Action Oriented Homework**_ –

   f. _**Relational Orientated Homework**_ –

Step 8 _Conjoin_ **the counselee(s) to the Body of Christ accordingly. According to this session choose what best fits for the counselee(s)**

a. _Membership_ – the counselee would be lead to join a local church that they may experience love and enjoy the blessings of God-honoring relationships .

b. _Maturity_ – the counselee would be lead to get involved in discipleship courses in a local church that would lead them into loving God, loving others on a consistent basis and living a life that reflects the character of Christ.

c. _Magnification_ – the counselee would be led to come to appreciate, value, and adore the character of God through heart-felt genuine worship of Him in a local church.

d. _Ministry_ – the counselee would be led to join a ministry where they can develop in bearing burdens and meeting needs according to the various relationships they will develop through the local church.

e. _Missions_ – the counselee would be led into supporting a local church in sharing and defending the Christian Faith

Case Report form (Here is an example)

Case Report Form
(NANC form with minor adaptations)

Counselor's Name _____   Name   of   Counselee_____

Date of Appt. _____   Session # _____

Time of Appt. _____

1. Significant background information

2. Summary of reason they came for counseling (presentation problem)

3. What changes were made by the counselee since last session (as a result of applying firs session's counsel and performing last session's homework)?

4. What main problem(s) were discussed in this session?

5. What unbiblical habits of thinking/behaving are you seeing in the counselee (pre-conditioning)?

6. What idols and lust of the heart are emerging? (I must have _____)

7. What biblical solutions were presented in this session (tie in with #4)?

8. What homework was given and how did it specifically apply to the problems (tie in with #4)?

9. If someone asked the counselee right after the session, "What did you learn that you needed to change?" what would you want him to say?

10. How was hope or encouragement given in this session?

11. How is the overall counseling process progressing and what issues have been sufficiently addressed by you and changed by the counselee?

12. What are your goals for future sessions?

If the session is not moving, review Jay Adam's "50 Failure Factors" at the back of the Christian Counseling Manual.

Bibliography

Adams, Jay. How to Help People Change, Grand Rapids: Zondervan, 1986.

Adams, Jay. Solving Marriage Problems, Grand Rapids: Zondervan, 1983.

Easron, M.G. Easton's Bible Dictionary (Logos Research System: reprint), Oak Harbour, WA" Public Domain, 1996.

Grudem, Wayne. Systematic Theology, Leicester: Inter-Varsity Press, 1994.

Lane, Timothy S. and Paul David Trip. How People Change, Greensboro, NC: New Growth Press, 2002.

Mack, Wayne. Various courses taught at the Master's College from 2000-2003.

Mac Arthur, John. Hard to Believe, Nashville: Thomas Nelson Inc.,2003.

Patten, Randy. Various workshops at the Counseling and Discipleship Trainings of the National Association of Nouthetic Counselors.

Powlison, David. Seeing With New Eyes, Phillipsburg, New Jersey: P&R Publishing, 2003.

Scott, Stuart. Various courses taught at the Master's College from 2000-2003.

Street, John. Various Courses taught at the Master's College from 2000-2003.

Thomson, Rich. The Heart of Man and The Mental Disorders, Houston: Biblical Counseling Ministries, Inc., 2004.

Tripp, Paul David. Instruments in the Redeemer's Hands: People in Need of Change Helping People in Need of Change, Phillipsburg, NJ: P&R Publ., 2002.

Varner, Ivory. Various teachings at Bible Way Fellowship Baptist Church, Houston Texas.

Warren, Rick. The Purpose Driven Church, Grand Rapids: Zondervan, 1995.

CPSIA information can be obtained
at www.ICGtesting.com
Printed in the USA
FSOW03n1309010515
6856FS